One of life's great charmers

First published 2015

Second revised and extended edition 2017

Mifair Publishing – Potters Bar, Herts, England

ISBN 978-0-9543967-3-2

Typeset in Times 11pt on 18pt

Design by Concept Design

Printed in England by CreateSpace, an Amazon.com company

Michael Fairley

One of life's great charmers

A biography of

Charles Kay

Sporting legend, songwriter and well-loved comedian
1870 – 1928

SECOND EDITION

Dedication

This book is dedicated to my mother, Dorothy Fairley, daughter of Charles and Florrie Kay, who never really new that much about her father. The internet and the availability of archived research information has enabled me to add considerably to what the family already knew. She would have been fascinated by how his life unfolded.

Front Cover

Caricature of Charles and Florrie Kay as the Trents in their performance of Detective Copp. Drawn in 1915

Contents

Preface

I never knew my grandfather, Charles Kay. He had parted from my grandmother, Florence Kay (nee Florence Lane), some twenty years before I was born. My mother, their daughter, spent much of her early life with her grandmother, Ada Lane – although she could recall being backstage at various times and peeping through the side curtains during some of their stage performances – before returning to live with her mother and new stepfather from the age of eight. A limited number of mementoes and photographs of Charles Kay, or Florence Kay, survived over the years, but he was seldom discussed in family circles. No contact appears to have been maintained with him after 1917.

It was only after both my own parents had passed away that I began to search for more information. I certainly knew that Charles and Florrie Kay had been on the stage together between 1913 and 1917, as well as the name of some of the skits and sketches that they performed, but little else. It was from this basic knowledge background that his extraordinary life story eventually began to evolve. And what a story it has proved to be.

The availability of *The Stage* Newspaper's on line archive soon began to reveal numerous references to Charles Kay from long before he teamed-up and married my grandmother, to some years after they had split up. Once details of theatres and dates performed began to unfold, it soon became possible to search annual census and local newspaper records in the British Newspaper Archive for more information, theatre reviews in *The Era* (a British weekly paper noted for its great theatrical coverage in the early 1900s) – and a whole host of other references to him in the British Library and newspaper archives in Australia.

Much to my surprise, it soon transpired that he was also an all-round sporting and concert hall legend across a wide range of different sporting and amateur theatrical activities in Devon in the later part of the 1800s and early 1900s, long before going on the professional stage. Furthermore, he was known at different periods under different names – from Charles Beachcroft Kay, to C B Kay and even C B K Beachcroft. It also evolved that he had even been awarded an Olympic gold medal under the later name for participation in the 1900 Summer Games in Paris.

Even more of a surprise was that he had already had three young 'wives', with eleven children between them, before he married my grandmother, as well as having numerous court appearances for everything from debt, trespass, poaching, bankruptcy, hotel licensing, and even abduction of a minor and child desertion. After parting from my grandmother, he went on to become engaged and/or 'married' to another young woman before finally emigrating to Australia, where he continued his career on the stage and then in radio.

This book is an attempt to bring together all of this rich history and background of Charles Kay – variously described as a charmer, charismatic, of impressive physic, a brilliant comedian and songwriter. It is hoped that readers will find it of interest.

Michael Fairley

Acknowledgements

It had always been a challenge to find historical information about Charles Kay, partly because there was not a great deal of family information to start with, partly as it turned out because during his life he went under quite a number of different names, and partly because of a lack of easily searchable resources.

It was only the continued development and availability of searchable archived information at the British Newspaper Archive, *The Stage* Archive, *The Era* archive, the UK Census, Australian Newspaper Archive, The British Library, Olympic records, Devon sporting records and various court records, that is was eventually possible to build a more detailed record of his life and activities. Thanks are due to all of these for their invaluable work in obtaining and preserving such historical records and making them available to the public and researchers.

Particular acknowledgement is made to the British Library Board for permission to reproduce various page images/clippings; to items included with permission of the British Newspaper Archive (www.britishnewspaperarchive.co.uk); to *The Stage* Archive (www.archive@thestage.co.uk) for permission to reproduce selected adverts mentioning Charles Kay; to The British Library for scanning and providing selected page images.

A list of newspapers and journals that were accessed through the British Newspaper Archive, *The Stage* Archive; The British Library; and the National Library of Australia can be seen in Appendix IV.

Charles Beachcroft 'Beachy' Kay
photographed for *'The Throne and Country'* journal
in August 1908.

Image © The British Library , LOU LON 24 (1908).

Charles Kay – One of life's great charmers

Son of a clergyman, accomplished sportsman, Olympic gold medallist, public house landlord, variety artist, song writer, comedian and humourist, pantomime villain, socialite – and serial adulterer.

Charles Kay, also known at various times as Charles Beachcroft Kay, C B Kay, Charles Beachy Kay Beachcroft, C B K Beachcroft, and even under the stage name of Jack Trent, was undoubtedly a larger than life character who seemed to excel at pretty-well everything that he did, whether at being a 'Gentleman of Independent means', a sporting legend who played at County level in cricket, hockey and rugby, an Olympic Gold Medallist, a respected baritone singer, acting as 'mine host' and entertainer at all kinds of local Devon charity and social events and venues, a regular gambler, landlord or licensee of various Devon public houses and, eventually, becoming a well-known Music Hall variety artist, song writer, comedian, actor and touring theatre company manager who played at venues throughout London and the UK, South Africa, Australia and New Zealand for more than twenty years.

Search through historical newspaper, magazine and theatre records from around 1885 to the mid-1920s and there hardly seems to be more than a month or two when he is not mentioned for either some sporting activity – whether cricket, hockey, rugby, football, lawn tennis, ice skating, roller skating, rowing, pigeon shooting, ping-pong, billiards, swimming, cycling, dog coursing – or for his various court appearances, for frequently being in the news as a

1

public house landlord, as well as for all kinds of highly praised amateur (in Devon) and professional theatre performances in London and the provinces, for regularly playing the Baron or Wicked Uncle in pantomimes, and still finding time to write numerous music hall songs, skits, sketches and shows.

In all these references he was regularly described as being the possessor of a fine appearance and splendid physique (noted in *The Era* as 'six foot of smartness'), as vigorous, fresh, charismatic, a great charmer, intensely funny, humorous, of having great natural ability, as being a mixture of dignity and impudence, certainly an excellent character impersonator, and a well-loved comedian who could put 'bottoms on seats' and fill theatres. He was undoubtedly very much a 'ladies man' who had a succession of very young 'wives' over a period of forty or so years – even to the extent of being charged with the abduction of a minor with the intention of having carnal knowledge – as well as having multiple children (at least 13) by his different wives/lady friends.

Mind you, he did have some setbacks during the almost 30 years in which he lived in Devon during the late 1800s and early 1900, including numerous appearances in court for everything from trespass, poaching, abduction, debt, entertainment licenses, bankruptcy, licensing objections from the Bishop of Exeter and from a Devon brewery, as well as very public divorce proceedings from at least one wife and desertion and child maintenance court appearances from a live-together partner.

It is then perhaps somewhat surprising to find that he was the son of Church of England vicar – not the expected family background for someone who could perhaps be described as a rather loveable rogue. He also had a number of uncles and other relatives by marriage, including well-established solicitors, barristers and pillars of Devon society. Certainly Charles Kay was part of a very well-known Devon family and fashionable society circle.

Performing on the amateur variety stage from the early 1890s and then on the professional stage from 1905 was perhaps a natural extension of his very eventful life. Initially going on the professional boards as *'The Typical Topical Talker'* and providing a humorous discourse or parody on events and activities of the time, and later going on to write and present his own successful skits, sketches or shows such as *'Do be Careful'*, *'Detective Copp'*, *'Kiss in the Ring'*, *'The Big Policeman and his Little Black Cat'*, *'The Simple Little Curate'*, *'Little Babette'* and *'The Allies'* musical, performing over the years with at least four different female 'partners'. He also created his own theatrical touring shows as well as managing and producing shows for leading theatre groups.

Successfully touring on the Stoll and Moss theatre circuit and also regularly playing the London halls, he went on to additionally become a well-respected annual performer playing the villain in Christmas Pantomimes around the UK that included *'Babes in the Wood'*, *'The House that Jack Built'*, *'Robinson Crusoe'*, *'Cinderella'*, and with performance runs of up to 15 weeks or more at many venues – perhaps an ideal opportunity to meet even more impressionable young ladies.

Charles Kay, later to change his name to Jack Trent for several years before emigrating (with another young lady) to Australia when the new world of cinema and silent films began to adversely affect bookings at the UK's variety theatres after World War I and into the early 1920s, and where he was to go on to successfully tour theatres in both that country and New Zealand for almost seven years (as well as still playing cricket), eventually dying from pneumonia in Melbourne in 1928.

He was undoubtedly very much of a 'one-off' personality – sometimes reported as eccentric or erratic – who made his mark on the Devon sporting, social, theatrical and venue scene before delighting audiences in theatres across England and Scotland for more than twenty years, followed by some 7 years performing on the stage and radio in Australia and new Zealand

It is certainly not very often that it is possible to document in so much detail the life of a late 19th and early 20th century character, and it is undoubtedly interesting to follow his family background and lifestyle through to understand how this somewhat charmed life all began and unfolded.

Born into church and fashionable society

Charles Beachcroft Kay was born in the Whip & Collar Public House, a 17th century coaching inn at Mill End, Rickmansworth, Nr. Watford, Hertfordshire in 1870, where his mother Elizabeth (Bessie), his father John, stepsister Anne and stepbrother Henry – both from his father's earlier marriage at the Parish Church, West Drayton, Middlesex, in February 1853 to Anne Lamb, eldest daughter of Henry Lamb of Salisbury Square, London – plus two servants, were in lodgings.

Charles was the son of a Church of England clergyman. His father, the Reverend John Lowder Kay, the third son of William Kay, a merchant of Grove House, Liverpool, had been born in Manchester in 1818. He matriculated at Magdalen College, Oxford, in 1838, obtained a BA in 1844 and an MA in 1846, and was ordained in 1851 by the Bishop of Chester, initially being assigned as a priest to the Church of St. Peter, Everton, Liverpool. He was later licensed by the Lord Bishop of Salisbury to the curacy of both St. Peter and Holy Trinity, Dorchester in 1858/59, at St Bartholomew, Sydenham, and in December 1873 as the Rector of Greatworth, a large parish in the County of Northampton with medieval settlements and incorporating the parishes of Stuchbury and Halse.

Other references to the Rev. J Lowder Kay can be found in 1865 when he is attending a grand dinner attended by local Conservatives at the Bull Inn, Dartford, to meet the Conservative candidate Lord Holmesdale. Then in September 1869 he is reported in the *Watford Observer* as reading the lesson at the Rickmansworth Parish Church Harvest Festival

Charles's mother, Elizabeth (more commonly known as Bessie), was the eldest surviving daughter of John and Susan Beachy of Beech Park, a six-bedroomed villa in two acres of grounds, including paddocks, in Highweek, a village of around 350 houses about one mile west of Newton Abbot, Devon. One of their nearest neighbours was Sir Samuel White Baker and Lady Baker. Sir Samuel was the great explorer of the Upper Nile, as well as being a J.P. for the county and a president of Newton College.

Elizabeth Beachy is noted in the local paper at the time of her marriage to John Lowder Kay as being 'accomplished', while her father is recorded in the 1871 Census as being a 'Landed proprietor'. One of her brothers was an Attorney.

The Beachy family was certainly well-known in Devon. Her uncle was a solicitor, while another relative is recorded as a barrister. The family home is shown as having four servants, including a 'Plain Cook', 'Parlourmaid' and 'Housemaid' – all at wages under £20, all found.

FASHIONABLE MARRIAGE AT HIGHWEEK. – On Tuesday last the parish was the source of much gaiety on the occasion of the marriage of the Rev. John Lowther Kay, of Sydenham, Kent, to Miss Bessie Beachy, the elder and accomplished daughter of J. Beachy Esq., of Beach Park, Newton Abbot. The interesting

Extract from the Exeter and Plymouth Gazette, August 2nd, 1867. Image © The British Library Board. All rights reserved. Included with permission of the British Newspaper Archive (www.britishnewspaperarchive.co.uk)

The marriage of the Rev. John Lowder Kay and Elizabeth Beachy had taken place in the Parish of Highweek on 30th July 1867, three years before Charles Beachcroft Kay was born. It was written up in some detail at this time in the *Exeter and Plymouth Gazette* under the heading of 'Fashionable Marriage at Highweek'.

The report stated that 'The interesting ceremony was performed by the Rev. S. G Harris, Vicar of the Parish, with the bride given away by her father. Miss Beachy wore a beautiful móire dress, with an elegant lace shawl, trimmed with Honiton lace sprigs, white chip bonnet ornamented with white May flowers and orange blossom intertwined. The happy couple left by the up mid-day train to spend their honeymoon abroad.'

Sadly, Charles's father died in February 1877 while he was still the Rector at Greatworth and when Charles was just seven years old, leaving a will finally sworn at £450. The will was proved on the 11th March, 1877 by William Henry Bateman Kay of Clifton, near Bristol – the nephew of Charles – and Louisa Kay, William's sister, of Tonbridge Wells, Kent. At that time, Charles's mother Elizabeth (Bessie) decided to move the family to Wolborough, a small ancient market parish on the north side of the River Lemon and one mile south west of Newton Abbot, Devon – and little over a mile from the village of Highweek where she had been born and grew up, and where her parents and other various family relatives still lived.

Elizabeth's mother died the following year, and her father in 1884. Her parent's family home at Beech Park was then sold and all the effects auctioned. These included engravings, oil paintings and pictures, over 300 volumes of books, silver plated goods, cut glass, as well as a 4-wheel pony carriage, pony, and a silver mounted harness. Probate was grated at a figure in excess of £6,000 (estimated at nearer £400,000 in today's values).

In the 1881 Census (and in *East & South Devon Advertiser*

newspaper reports up to at least 1885) Bessie Kay, now shown as Bessie Kay Heaton, and her family (Charles and the stepbrother and stepsister) were still living in Wolborough – at 1 Belgrave Terrace. The young Charles attended Newton Abbot Proprietary College, a relatively small, but successful, public school in the town which was to later be renamed as Newton Abbot College, and was claimed to be one of the best in the West of England, as well as one of the leading educational establishments in the whole country.

It certainly had distinguished Council members and Patrons. President of the School Council was the Earl of Devon who presented prizes at the annual prize-giving, at which regular attenders were the likes of Admiral Cornish-Bowden, General Reynell Taylor (General of the Indian Army until he retired in 1877), General Riach and Dowager Lady Haldon, while prayers were given by the Bishop of Exeter.

The College had both borders and day students and was said to provide sound classical and hematical instruction side by side with essential education subjects – physical science, English language and history, and with a special acquaintance with the best English writers. Subjects that would eventually stand him in good stead in both the amateur and professional theatrical worlds he was to later move into – although it was the legal profession that the family had originally planned for him and which he had initially studied and passed the examinations for. He was also listed amongst the successes achieved in the 1886 Cambridge Local examinations by boys from Newton College.

The College was also strong on sports, students encouraged to play rugby, hockey and cricket. Indeed, after leaving Newton College he was soon playing rugby for Totnes Rugby Club. Rowing, swimming and cycling also seemed to be part of his life. All these activities were to feature large in his development into a very charismatic country gentleman. Somewhere along the line he also learns to excel in shooting. Cricket however, is undoubtedly where he was to have many successful playing years at local, County and Olympic level – at times being referred to as the W G Grace of Devon.

A cricketing legend is born

Even before leaving Newton College in the summer of 1886, Charles Kay – now widely and more affectionately known and reported in Devon newspapers as C B Kay – was playing cricket at both first and second XI level for the College. By the autumn of that year he had formed his own challenge cricket team, and was playing matches against a wide variety of local Newton and Devon teams.

The 11th September 1886 edition of the *East & South Devon Advertiser* for example, reports on Mr. C B Kay's XI beating Newton Juniors by 26 runs

Although no longer an official student at the College, C B Kay continued to play in games for the College. In a report from May 1887, Kay was noted as the opening bat for the College in a game against South Devon. The College side included students, masters and past students. The game ended in victory for the College by 12 runs. Scores were said to be low on account of splendid bowling by both sides.

Also in May of that year, Newton College played a match against Mannamead School, which resulted in a victory for the College – a game in which C B Kay scored 48 runs. The same month he is recorded as playing for Newton Town against Bovey Tracey, in which the visitors were defeated by 53 runs. It was said that 'Kay and Sandilands played thoroughly good cricket for their 36 and 37 respectively.' Then, in the June, Kay plays again against Bovey Tracey, but this time playing for Newton College. In July of that year, Kay is once more playing for the College against Newton

Football Club on the College grounds, where he scored 20 in a match that resulted in a draw.

August 1887 now shows C B Kay playing for Newton College Present in a match against Newton College Past. It was noted that Kay played an admirable innings of 109 for the Present team, but that the game was brought to an abrupt conclusion, rain stopping play after five wickets. The same month Mr. C B Kay's XI plays against Newton Colts. Mr. Kay's XI winning by an innings and 116 runs, and then in a match where he played for South Devon in a cricket match against the Plymouth Garrison, in which the Garrison won by 8 wickets. However, he is still playing for Newton College as late as June 1888.

At the Annual Supper of Newton cricket Club in November 1888, one member of the Club (C B Kay) was announced as the winner of the prize for the highest average during the season. He was also the winner of the highest individual score. However, according to Club rules, one member was not allowed to take both prizes. Kay therefore elected to take the prize for the highest score. Although still only 18, he has by now also been elected to the Committee of the Club.

Numerous newspaper reports of cricket matches in which Kay played, and played well, continue through the late 1880s and into the 1890s. June 1890 for example sees him playing for South Devon against the Gondoliers, a game which resulted in a win for the home team by 56 runs. C B Kay was said to have played a good game. In the September, Kay is playing for Dawlish Cricket Club against a team from Paignton. Dawlish batted first, Kay scoring 45 runs out of a total of 89 for the side. Paignton had scored 59 for four at the call of time at 6.00 pm.

At the end of the 1890 season Newton Cricket Club were able to announce that they had played 12 games, winning six, losing four and drawing two. C B Kay once again topped the Club's batting averages. At the same time, they reported that Newton Colts cricket team had played 16 matches, winning 10 and losing six. Mr. Kay, the Colt's captain, again topped the batting averages.

The following year the Club played 10 matches, winning four, losing five and drawing one. Press reports stated that C B Kay had been in fine form with the bat throughout the whole season, scoring 240 runs and having an average of 30 runs per innings. The highest individual score of 78 had also been by Kay. This was in a match against Chudleigh in which it was said that 'Kay played a brilliant innings for his 78 not out and during the whole of which he did not give a single chance.'

In August 1895 two Newton cricketers, H Francis and H B Mapleton, were reported in the *East & South Devon Advertiser* as completing their 1,000 runs, with C B Kay following closely behind on 970, while a report in the same newspaper in the following month stated that the Newton Cricket Club had reported that the season had been more successful than could have been anticipated. Of the eight matches played, five had been won. It was noted that C B Kay batted well in every match and was far ahead of any of the other players in the year's batting averages.

August 1896 sees Kay playing for Dawlish v Montpelier (Master's XI) in which he clean bowled eight men for 23 runs and then scored 20 runs. Dawlish won by 38 runs. It was reported that 'Kay had not done anything in the bowling line since leaving Newton College, where he was a fast but somewhat erratic bowler.'

A report in the *East & South Devon Advertiser* in July 1899, noted that whilst playing for Dawlish against Netherton, Mr C B Kay scored 119 not out – including five 4's and seventeen 3's.

His love for cricket – at both a local and County level – appears on numerous occasions over the coming years, both as a player and an organiser. He was regarded as a renowned batsman in the early days of Dawlish cricket and later went on to score two centuries for South Devon and one for Torquay. In local games he was to total in excess of 1,000 runs in successive seasons. In the early days of the Dawlish Cricket Club he was also elected to the Committee. He was said to be a great character and a prolific run getter for Exeter, yet was happy to help out his local team on occasions.

More will be mentioned of his cricket prowess as other chapters unfold. Suffice to say that as CB Kay, C B Kay Beachcroft, or Charles Kay, he played regular cricket for 19 years, representing Devon at County level, England at Olympic level, whilst also playing for local teams throughout the County (and then later continuing to play into his 50s after emigrating to Australia), as well as being a Devon County rugby football player and a Devon County hockey forward. He was a prolific scorer at cricket over the years, and is said to have scored well over 17,000 runs during his playing career, including 15 centuries and 85 scores of between 50 and 100, as well playing a total of 126 not out innings. He was also a Hertfordshire cricketer where he had his birth qualification.

An unexpected marriage

While finding time for his beloved cricket and a whole host of other sporting activities, Charles Kay had also found time to marry a local 18-year old girl, Rose Isabella Serjeant, on the 11th September 1889 at the Exeter registry office. He was aged just 19 at the time. Rose's parents were shown in various press reports as being in charge of the Gentleman's Club in Queen Street, Exeter (which he apparently frequented), while Charles was also recorded as being the nephew of the late Henry G Beachy, a successful Newton Abbot solicitor, who had placed money into trust for him.

It was reported in a number of local papers that 'the unexpected marriage had caused a great deal of gossip in the town.' The couple lived in Exeter after the marriage. Perhaps not unsurprisingly given the local gossip, his new wife gave birth to a daughter on the 21st January 1890 – just four months after they had been married. The birth took place at the Royal Hotel in Dawlish, a venue he was to have quite a long and somewhat unfortunate association with.

The 1891 Census shows him now living back in Wolborough, at 1 Gloucester Terrace, and his occupation as 'Living on his own means.' Certainly there seems to have been money in the Beachy family. His uncle, John Beachy, left some £27,000 in his estate – quite a sum in the late 1800s (close to £1.7 million today) – some of which had been placed in trusts for Charles, his mother and Miss Isabel Beachy, 21, together with £1,112.16s (now around £60,000 from the sale of Beachcroft's own house in 1895).

Unfortunately for Charles, the sole trustee (a George Furneaux, wine merchant of London, but living in Newton Abbot) dealing with the various trusts and property money was to eventually end up at the Devon Winter Assizes held at Exeter charged with 'intent to defraud, convert, or appropriate the trust property for his own use and benefit, and did otherwise dispose of the property.' Furneaux had been a solictor's clerk with Richard Beachy, solicitor and son of the testator, and therefore should have had some legal knowledge. In a report in the *East & South Devon Advertiser*, 9th February 1901 it was stated that the prisoner's gross liabilities were £27,000, with assets of only £581.

Defending the accused, Mr. Lawrence, told the court that Furneaux blamed his difficulties on the fact that Mrs. Heaton and her son, Beachcroft, had made incessant money demands upon him. He also said that Beachcroft was first articled to a lawyer, then had become a comedian, at which he had failed, and 'was always without money, constantly asking the prisoner for more, later adding that the condition of the estate was largely due to the incessant and excessive demands of Mrs. Heaton, whose income was not sufficient to meet her wants, and whose condition had been extremely aggravated by the reckless and extravagant career of her son Beachcroft.'

Despite the prisoner trying to blame Mrs. Heaton and Beachcroft for his problems, the Western Times report of the case in February 1901 stated that Mr. Justice Darling in his summing up, had said that 'the prisoner (the trustee) had made away with the money and there was no means of saying where it had gone except that it went into his bank account, and there was no proof that it came out, except for the benefit of himself.' The prisoner had not lost only their money but his own as well.' His Lordship sentenced Furneaux to 14 months imprisonment.

Over the period of five years after his marriage Charles and Rose Kay went on to have four children in fairly quick succession: Margaret Bessie Beachy Kay in 1890, Frederick Charles Kay in September 1892, Florence Kay in February 1894 and Henry Aubrey Kay in October 1895.

However, being married and having four children in five years didn't seem to slow down any of Kay's sporting (or gambling) activities. In March 1889, when Kay was still only 19, he took part in a billiards match at Newton Liberal Club that had been organised between himself and a Mr. W J Norris. The game was for 100 up, Kay beating his opponent by four points in the first game, but with Norris beating Kay by 32 in the second tournament. Kay then promptly challenged Norris to play him in a game of 250 up. This challenge was accepted. The match was all even until the last 50, Norris eventually winning by just 19 points.

In a billiards match played at the Albert Hotel, Dawlish, in April 1893, between members of the Dawlish and Newton Conservative Clubs, Dawlish won by 25 points. Kay was one of three players that scored 100 for Newton.

A year later, Newton and Dawlish Conservative Clubs again played a friendly billiards match at Dawlish in the first week of March 1894, the Dawlish team winning by 80 points. Mr. C B Kay, playing for Newton, scored 100 points.

In another report from June 1890 Mr. Gage Hodge's famous pack of other hounds met at Newton Abbot station. The meet was exceedingly grand with a field that included ladies and gentlemen from all parts of Devon. The weather was fine, though a little dark at the start. The hounds – eight couple and a brace of terriers – were taken by train in charge of Arthur Mason, kennel huntsman. The conditions left nothing to be desired, and as they trotted through the bottom part of Newton a lot of townsfolk joined the hunt, including Mr. C B Kay.

The hounds on being cast off made good the various leats and other water-courses, and then commenced to draw steadily up the Teign. Snatches of scent were had at different landing places and the field were in good spirits at the news that 'spurs' had been spotted a little higher up, but to no avail.

The lower portion of the Bovey river was drawn, the Leat, and more of the Teign, yet no trail was struck. The day, although proving blank, was splendidly enjoyable.

Then, in late October 1890, playing in what was described as 'The most exciting rugby match ever seen during the season' between Newton College and Rev. G H Knights XV, Kay is noted as meeting with a most regrettable accident, and was obliged to retire from the game. The local newspaper report described this as follows: 'In collaring Pinsent, the College back, two of Kay's fingers on the right hand were violently forced apart, and the hand split open in a fearful manner. Some time must elapse before the wound can heal.'

By now Charles was also already developing something of a reputation as an amateur singer, theatrical entertainer and organizer, indeed had become a founder member and manager of the newly formed Newton Variety Theatre. By April 1891 *The Exeter and Plymouth Gazette* had noted that Charles Kay applied to the Newton Police Court for two theatrical licenses – one for the Dolphin Hotel, Bovey Tracy, and one for the Town Hall, Chudleigh – so that he could organize local performances. Both licenses were granted.

However, not all is going well for him (as some of the following court appearances indicate) for just a few months later, Charles Beachy Kay and Edward Loudes, another minister's son, are summoned by Felix John Harris, a local gamekeeper, for unlawfully trespassing in pursuit of game (poaching). The gamekeeper stated that he saw the defendants in his grounds with four dogs and an air gun. The defence was that the two of them were only hunting for rats, upon which the Bench dismissed the case.

There is little doubt that he was a crack shot, as he won innumerable prizes at pigeon shooting over the years, including several in big sweepstakes at the Welsh Harp, Hendon, and also the Torquay and Ashbury Challenge Cups.

Apart from being on the Committee of the cricket club and the secretary of the Variety Theatre, he was also elected the treasurer of the Newton Association Football Club at a formation meeting held in April 1893.

Another court case in January 1894 sees Charles Kay once more being summoned, this time for trespassing on the railway line at Newton Abbott. It was stated that he had been returning home by train from singing in a concert in Teignmouth and afterwards attending a ball. The train arrived back at his station at 3.16 a.m. It was said that he left the train and instead of crossing the bridge to the station exit, he instead crossed the rails, paying no head to an Inspector Tucker's calls. In judgement, the Bench considered that passengers should all obey the bye laws. He was fined the princely sum of £1.00, including costs.

There is also a report of a Norton tailor's judgement summary against Mr. C B Kay for the recovery of £22 0s 0d for clothes supplied coming before the Norton County Court in December 1896; another summons against Mrs. Kay for a debt of £3 10s by the Norton Gas Company, was also on the list. Both came before the Registrar at the Court, were admitted and settlements effected.

In June 1894, the *East & South Devon Advertiser* runs a report on the Conservative 'At Home' held at the Market Buildings, which was attended by a large and influential gathering. Decorations for the event had been carried out on an elaborate scale, the interior of the building undergoing quite a transformation, changing from the prosaic meeting place for butter women, into a charming spot the like of which was never before seen in the centre of a town the size of Newton. From the walls and roof hung hundreds of flags and trophies, and when the building was illuminated by the thousand and one fairy lamps and Chinese lanterns the sight was extremely pretty and pleasing. Visitors came from across East and South Devon. Mr. & Mrs. C B Kay were identified in the newspaper as being amongst the influential gathering.

Founding pioneer of Newton Abbot Cycling Club

In May 1889 a meeting was held at the Globe Hotel, Newton Abbot, to look at the feasibility of forming a cycling club for the town. The meeting agreed a club was needed and that this should be called The Newton Abbot Rovers Cycling Club. Officers for the formation of a committee were then elected, with Mr. C B Kay (Charles Kay) being appointed the Hon. Secretary.

The first annual supper of the Club was held on the 23rd January 1890 at the Colwill's Commercial Hotel, Newton Abbot (since demolished and now an office block), with about 50 persons present. Mr. Seale-Hayne, M.P., President of the club occupied the chair. Mr. C B Kay was present as the Hon. Secretary. It was reported that the room in which the supper was held was very prettily decorated with evergreens, draping, fairy lamps, and flags, and the presence of a bicycle on the wall immediately in front of the Chairman, in illustration of the club's motto, 'Success to the Bicycle Club,' completed a picture at once effective and suitable. The repast itself was said to be of an excellent character

In October 1890 a very successful cycle carnival, organized by Kay, was held at Newton by members of the Rovers Cycling Club

> ### Cycle Carnival at Newton.
> A very successful cycle carnival was held at Newton on Tuesday evening by members of the Rovers Cycling Club assisted by contingents from the Exeter, Torquay, Torre, Torbay, Paignton, Teignmouth, Dart Vale, and London Athletic clubs. Surprising interest was manifest in the event by the public, and the attendance of spectators in the streets was quite phenomenal.

The East and South Devon Advertiser, 25th October, 1890. Image © The British Library Board. All rights reserved. Included with permission of the British Newspaper Archive (www.britishnewspaperarchive.co.uk)

assisted by contingents from Exeter, Torquay, Torre, Torbay, Paignton, Teignmouth, Dart Vale and London Athletic clubs. Surprising interest was manifested in the event by the public, and the attendance of spectators in the streets was quite phenomenal. The carnival was eagerly looked forward to by sightseers and riders as well, with the 'wheelers' of Newton involved with the utmost readiness and enthusiasm. The *East and South Devon Advertiser* report on the carnival was quite comprehensive as the following extract shows.

'The procession was announced to start from the Market Hall at half-past seven but owing to the late arrival of some of the riders there was a considerable delay, at which the dense crowd outside began to show signs of impatience and considerably enlivened matters by keeping up a continual rat tat upon the door. This led to Sergeant Tucker and several other 'members of the force' being sent for, and on their arrival the disorder ceased, but it still seemed an utter impossibility to get the procession through the crowd, which was becoming thicker and thicker in the Market Place. Meanwhile the riders inside were lighting up and completing their preparations.

'Most of the disguises adopted were perfectly inscrutable, while some made no pretence at hiding their identity. Nevertheless, Mr. C B Kay (Hon. Sec) was most strikingly made up by Mr. Padey Pennington (a well-known stage performer who was not averse to organising public stunts, and who had performed at the Alexandria Hall the night before where it was said that his experiments in hypnotism kept the audience in roars of laughter for over an hour) to represent Mephistopheles, his blood red garb and fiendish face giving him a very strange appearance. Mr. W R Churchill, as a wild

Indian, was most elaborately decked out, and indeed was one of the best of the whole lot, whilst Mr. Padey Pennington came out disguised as Bill Adams, the 'real hero' of Waterloo. His illuminations consisted of a dilapidated stable lantern hoisted behind on a broomstick.

'At length they were ready and filed out of the hall and proceeded through a narrow passage in the crowd to the Drum Clock. Here the people were thicker still, and there were several spills in rounding the corner into Queen Street. The route proceeded round the town and back to head-quarters at Colwill's Commercial Hotel. Hundreds watched the procession go by from windows.

'There was a display of fireworks throughout the ride, the cyclists having provided themselves with an abundance of coloured lights. The spectacle was both picturesque and amusing, and appeared to be greatly appreciated by the spectators.'

A smoking concert was afterwards held at the Hotel. Some excellent recitations were given, and a very convivial evening was spent.'

There seems little doubt that Charles Kay and Padey Pennington were well known to each other and that Pennington would have encouraged Kay's theatrical aspirations and sporting interests. Pennington was variously described over many years in West Country newspaper reports as being a variety entertainer, humorist, illustrious mimic, ventriloquist, musical artist, celebrated mind reader and clever hypnotist, and was said to have visited Newton so many times during the late 1880s and 1890s that he was very well-known in the neighborhood.

He was also a record holding athlete, who regularly challenged well-known figures in a race over 100 yards – which he always won. This would also have appealed to Charles Kay. It is also possible that Kay was helping to write some of the comic songs for Pennington, as well as the many musical pieces he wrote for his own performances on the amateur stage.

At the Annual General Meeting of the Cycling Club held at Colwill's Commercial Hotel with a large attendance in January 1891, Mr. C B Kay, the Hon. Secretary, read a report on the proceedings and activities during the 1890 season. He stated that the Club now had some 50 members and that during the season there had been 40 official cycling club runs. Mr. W Leatt won the gold medal for best attendance, having ridden 2,447 miles. Mr. Kay had cycled the second longest distance having ridden 2,084 miles. Mr. Kay was re-elected as the Club secretary.

February 1891 saw Newton Rovers Cycling Club hold their first 'Smoker' at their headquarters on a Wednesday night. Among the singers in the capital programme organised by the secretary, Mr. C B Kay was encored for singing *'They're after me'*, and *'He hadn't been used to luxuries'*. Later in the programme he came back and sang *'In Darkest London'*.

A few months later, at a regular meeting of the Club in April 1891, there was a good discussion on the merits of different types of bicycle tyres. It was announced that many members had gone in for 'cushioned' tyres, two members had changed to the 'Clincher Pneumatic' (the first detachable pneumatic tyre patented in 1890 by William K Bartlett) and 'Holborn Safety' tyres. The secretary, Mr.

C B Kay reported that he was sticking with his 'Singer Safety' tyre, but had also had 'Clincher Pneumatic' tyres fitted with great success. These were said to provide an increase in speed for the more serious cyclists and racers.

Charles Kay's cycling adventures were not always successful as the *Western Times* of the 5th October 1891 carried news that 'On Friday evening, Mr. C B Kay, the well-known bicyclist, whilst returning from Torquay on his machine was run into by a baker's cart and violently thrown to the ground. Besides a severe shaking he had his thumb dislocated. His bicycle was smashed almost beyond repair.'

Much later, in June 1895, while cycling back to Newton from Teignmouth with a Mr. C B Carlyle, his colleague met with s serious bicycle accident. In descending Ware Hill just before reaching Kingsteignton, the tyre of one of the wheels on Carlyle's bicycle came off and the rider lost control of the machine and was thrown off, receiving severe cuts about the head and face besides being considerably shaken. 'Mr. C B Kay helped Mr. Carlyle into Newton, where he was attended by a medical man and is now progressing as well as can be expected.'

Unfortunately, not all went well for the Cycling Club. A meeting of the club was held on the 22nd April 1892 at Mr. Robert's Cycle Stores in Union Street. It was proposed at this meeting by Mr. R J Butland, the hon. treasurer and seconded by Mr. Kay the hon. secretary: 'That owing to lack of interest in the welfare of the club displayed by its members, the meeting was of the opinion that steps should be immediately taken to wind up the club.' After much discussion, the motion was carried unanimously. A committee was then appointed to carry out the details in connection with abolishing the club.

As an aside to Kay's cycling ventures, a few years later in 1898, the East and South Devon Advertiser reported that Mr. C B Kay Beachcroft of the Royal Hotel Dawlish, whist returning from Exeter on his bicycle, came into violet collision with a novice riding on the wrong side of the road at Countess Weir Bridge. Mr. Beachcroft sustained a severe fracture of his collar bone, and his machine was badly damaged.

Newton Variety Company established

After finishing his studies at Newton College in 1886, Charles Kay was soon – as described in other chapters – actively and enthusiastically engaged in numerous sporting activities – including football, rugby, hockey, ice hockey, roller skating, cricket, cycling, lawn tennis, billiards and swimming and yet, at the same time, manages to find time to become involved within the world of local amateur theatricals and stage performances, as many of the reports from the 1890s display. Indeed, he becomes one of the leading figures in the establishment in early 1891, of the Newton Variety Company.

Already by December 1890, at just 20 years of age, Kay's comic character songs were said to have been very heartily appreciated by a large audience attending a Smoking Concert at the Commercial Hotel in Newton, and all his songs, which included *'The Grave Digger,'* and *'I dreamt that I was dreaming,'* all received encores.

Kay also participated in an entertainment in aid of H.M.S. Serpents Widows' and Orphans' Fund by members of the Newton Constitutional and Liberal Clubs on the 9th December. The ship, a torpedo cruiser, had entered service in 1888, but had run aground of Cape Vilan in northwest Spain on the 10th November during a heavy storm, with the loss of all but three of the 176 crew. Kay appeared in the entertainment as part of an Ethiopian quartette with W H Hugo, J Kerslake and Frank Williams as 'The Four Crows.' There was laughter in general throughout the performance, which was said to be ludicrous in the extreme. 'Each one of the quartette conducted themselves with crow-like solemnity, and with a studied seriousness that would have done credit to a young heir at his old

27

uncle's funeral.' The whole thing was a decided success.

In the same month he participates in an highly successful social evening at the Newton Constitutional Club, where a large number of members were present to see him in a capital get-up and being loudly applauded for the way he sang *'She's the Boss, and I'm the Slave.'* It's likely that these three concerts in December 1890, undoubtedly encouraged by Padey Pennington, seem to have prompted Charles Kay to join other likeminded persons in forming the Newton Variety Company in the following month – with almost immediate success.

In the February of 1891, the *East & South Devon Advertiser* reported that Broadhempston village had been 'electrified out of its usual dullness' on the evening of 6th February, by one of the best entertainments – if not the best – ever held in the place. The entertainment was provided by members of the newly formed Newton 'Star Variety' Company, and was witnessed by a highly appreciative audience.

Mr. Kay sang a capital comic song *'Where did you get that hat?'* in character, which created great amusement, and on being loudly encored he gave *'He hadn't been used to luxuries,'* in which he introduced several original verses alluding to local personages, which evidently were greatly appreciated and hit the mark.

In the second part of the programme Kay appeared on the stage extravagantly attired in the same Mephistopheles (a medieval legend and a subordinate to the devil) get-up that he used at the cycling carnival, and again sang *'I dreamt that I was dreaming,'* and being vociferously encored gave *'Comin through the Dye.'* The programme was eventually brought to a close by Messrs. Kay and H Kempe Hambly singing *'The wild man of Borneo,'* which was loudly encored.

By the March of 1891, C B Kay is now reported in *The East & South Devon Advertiser* as one of the outstanding players in two evenings of amateur theatricals performed by the newly formed Variety Company at the Newton Constitutional Club by local artists.

This event attracted greater interest than many professional stage plays. On the first of the evenings the members were invited to bring their lady friends, and such was the opportunity taken by the audience, that they were composed almost entirely of the fair sex, and some difficulty was experienced in accom-modating the large number that attended.

The third part of this amateur theatrical extravaganza consisted of a new burlesque written by local gentlemen, entitled *'The Babes and the Bogie man'*. For the occasion a sprinkling of clever and mirth provoking local hits written by Mr. C B Kay, were introduced into the piece. The steam roller, as a matter of course, formed the subject of one of the jokes, and the improvements

One of Kay's regular characters was to appear as Mephistopheles.

29

Amateur Theatricals at Newton

Amateur theatricals, when performed by local artists, usually attract greater interest than professional stage plays. Proof of this was forthcoming on Monday and Tuesday evenings, the occasion of the annual entertainments of the Constitutional Club. On the first of these evenings members were invited to bring their lady friends, and to such an extent was advantage taken of the opportunity that the audience composed almost entirely of the fair sex, and some difficulty was experienced in accommodating the large number who attended. On Tuesday the programme was repeated

The East and South Devon Advertiser, Saturday 7th March, 1891. Image © The British Library Board. All rights reserved. Included with permission of the British Newspaper Archive (www.britishnewspaperarchive.co.uk)

around the Oak Tree another. The lamp post erected outside the station also came in for a few lines of satire..

The female characters in the burlesque – Sarah Jane and Mary Ann, the King's sisters (described as two giddy young things, who were more than seven) – were very successfully taken by Mr. Charles B Kay and Mr. H Kempe Hambly, whose makes-up were decidedly novel. 'Mr. Kay, who has rapidly gained high repute in the town and neighbourhood as a comic singer of no ordinary merit, showed himself equally clever as a play-actor. Mr. Kay possesses abundant confidence, and his style is very 'taking.' His song, *'Sweet Seventeen,'* was most enthusiastically encored, and the character throughout was most cleverly sustained.'

The piece of the evening was perhaps the duet by Messrs. Kay and Hambly entitled *'The Sister's Frilling,'* which was vociferously encored, and the trio by Messrs. Kay, Hambly, and Greenslade, singing *'Up to Date,'* also met with loud applause. A grand concert finale, followed by a patriotic song and chorus, *'England, Home and Victory'* sung in a spirited way by Mr. Charles B Kay, concluded the performance.

Within a couple of weeks of the Constitutional Club

performances, the recently formed Newton Variety Company provided capital entertainment on the second day of a Grand Fancy Fair at Newton – the first day being a chess tournament with living pieces to raise funds for new fittings and furniture to the rooms of the Church Institute, and secondly to raise an additional classroom at All Saint's Mission Room.

The variety performances on the second day were held in an improvised concert room and were attended by a large and delighted audience. During the first part of the concert, C B Kay sang *'They're after me,'* and *'Up-to-date,'* as well as a comic duet song with Mr. H Kempe Hambly entitled *'The wild man of Borneo.'* In the second part of the concert Mr. Kay sang *'Where did you get that hat?'* and *'Comin through the Dye.'*

Then in April 1891, a grand entertainment was given by the Newton Variety Company at the Board School room, Broadhempston, an old Devon village founded in Saxon times. Mr. C B Kay appeared in the character of 'Good old mother Shipton,' in which he made some capital prophecies, the audience joining most heartily in the chorus. Mr. Kay, whose costume was most suitable, was of course encored and as a reply gave his very clever song entitled *'Up to Date.'*

The first part of the programme was brought to a close by Mr. Kay singing the comic song *'Then you wink the other eye,'* his costume being admirably suited to his encore *'I'm sweet seventeen.'*

Just a few weeks later, the Newton Variety Company performed *'The Bogie Man'* to a large audience at Chudleigh Town hall where Mr.Charles B Kay was the recipient of a very flattering ovation at the conclusion of each of his well rendered comic songs, which were given in character. *'He hadn't been used to luxuries'* and *'Good old mother Shipton'* were the titles of his songs, and in response to loud encores he gave *'All through a woman with coal black eyes'* and *'Hi boys! Hi boys! Come with your uncle Joe.'*

Another marked success of the evening was Mr Kay's rendering of *'Then you wink the other eye'* which was encored three times in succession, and was generally voted the smartest song of the evening. The following evening the same company performed practically the same programme at the Dolphin Hotel, Bovey Tracey, and were again successful in giving entire satisfaction.

In May 1891, a highly successful concert in aid of the Fife and Drum Band was given at the Alexandra Hall (built in 1871 as the Corn Exchange), Newton Abbot, on Monday by the Fife and Drum Band assisted by other ladies and gentlemen. Mr. C B Kay supplied the comic element and was a great success as the long and loud applause and series of *'Core'*, *'Core'*, *'Core'* abundantly testified.

'Hush the Brokers Man' was also sung by him with great effect, and as an encore he gave his ever popular *'Comin' through the Dye'* in which he introduced a special verse on Newton's Scapegoat, Albert Daymond, which fairly brought the house down. His next song was *'Get your hair cut'* in which he had scored such success at Torquay Theatre a fortnight before, which needless to say brought him another encore. In response, he gave *'A pity to waste it'* which vastly pleased the audience.

Wonderful character impersonator

May 1891 sees one of the best, in fact said to be the best, social concerts ever given at the Newton Constitutional Club, which was enjoyed by a large and appreciative audience on the Friday evening. Mr. C B Kay was reported in the *East & South Devon Gazette* of 9th May as being the hero of the evening as regards to vigour, freshness, ease and originality of character. 'Mr. Kay singing *'He hadn't been used to luxuries,'* was one of the most successful rendered pieces of the evening.' The report added that 'We are almost at a loss how fairly to describe his accomplishments. 12 months ago he was a good comic amateur but now, however, he is a good professional comic. The rapid and marked development he has made in this department not only bespeaks great natural ability, but a wonderful aptitude to impersonate character. His ease and gentlemanly deportment, and his facial contortions either to be gay or sad are so thoroughly at his command that he can be anything and everything at his will. This he demonstrated in rendering the comic song below, with the result that the company thought as he did, and felt as he did, only with this difference that he allowed them to laugh whilst he was sad and grieved sorely when he sang the following pathetic lines (his own composing) as an instance of his personal experience:

> *'Dear Newton Bells, sweet Tower Bells,*
> *We love to hear them chiming.*
> *But 'tween me and you one thing is true,*
> *You never hear them chiming.*
> *Newton folks put then there for the Jubilee,*

Thought when they all rang there'll be harmony;

Now the committee must feel very sad,

For whenever they play there's no tune at all.

Chorus

We haven't been used to luxuries.

Such bells we never tried;

The bells are crazy, the tunes are hazy,

And we could have cried! We cried!'

These last lines elicited much laughter, and in response to a hearty encore Mr. Kay sang another comic song *'Tis a pity to waste it,'* amid renewed encores.

The second in a series of winter socials was held at the Newton Constitutional Club in the October of 1891. Ladies were invited, and they responded in such numbers that not only was the room (capable of holding several hundred) filled to excess, but the approaches thereto and the billiard rooms, were all thronged with members and their friends.

One local newspaper report commented: 'Mr. C B Kay, Hon. Secretary of the social evening department, even if he could have anticipated such a recognition of his past indefatigable efforts, would hardly have been more successful in his arrangements, either by regard to his own inimitable performance as a comic, or in the talent array of local musical and vocal members who supported him.

'Kay in his comic character sang *'I'm selling up the 'appy',* *'appy', ome'* was exceedingly clever and funny, so funny, that the audience laughed themselves into an encore, which Mr. Kay complied by giving another humorous offering.

The following month, in early November 1891, Kay is first reported as attending a concert in aid of the Broadhempston church organ. Mr. C B Kay sang four very humorous songs in character, *'The shop walker,' 'Get your hair cut,' 'I'm not,'* and *'I'm selling up the 'appy,' 'appy' 'ome.'* All the songs were very entertaining.

A week or so later, at the third Social evening of the Newton Constitutional Club, Mr. Kay sang *'Break it gently,'* his get-up 'being very extravagant,' and the song rendered in good professional style, affording any amount of amusement. Mr. Kay later gave another comic song, *'Hi Boys, Hi Boys, come and join Uncle Joe,'* which was quite equal to his first effort, and was rapturously encored. Mr. Kay responded, giving another laughable song, *'Leathery Breaches.'*

Also in November, at another Social Evening at the Newton Constitutional Club, the *East and South Devon Advertiser* reported that Mr. Kay's efforts, especially *'Randy Pandy,'* vastly pleased the audience which, by the way they joined in the chorus, bid fair to be the song of the day, as it seems to please all classes.

In a fitting end to a year of variety theatre, several Newtonians, by invitation, visited Coombeinteignhead (Coombe-in-Teignhead), a village in South Devon, to assist the inhabitants at a concert in aid of their Reading Room. Mr. Kay sang four 'screamers' telling of his troubles consequent on the unauthorised growth of his hair, the unruly behaviour of his lodgers who would not 'be shifted.' As an encore he gave *'In'* and the story of the sale of his *'Appy 'ome.'* Mr.

Kay and Mr. Hambly also appeared as two Costers and sang *'Round the Town'* with great success, the encore 'betting' verse being very amusing.

The East and South Devon Advertiser, 19th March, 1892.

A ladies night at the Constitutional Club followed in February 1892. With a large audience and a capital programme, Mr. C B Kay came out very strong, singing in character two or three racy new songs and introducing in one of them some verses on the political meeting at the Alexandra Hall the previous evening and in which a *'monkey on a stick'* played a conspicuous part. This reference to the monkey seems to have caused some local discussion as Kay followed this up by placing a letter in the local *East and South Devon Advertiser* newspaper in which he stated that he would not 'hit' on a subject if the person was present.

The following month again saw a highly successful evening at the Norton Constitutional Club. Attended by a large audience, the evening was highly successful. Mr. C B Kay told the company in melodious accents that *'They went to the usual place,'* also that *'Them don't speak to one another now,'* and gave the highly sentimental ditty *'Oh! 'ampsted.'* His efforts meeting with the strong approval of the audience, Mr. Kay obliged with encores, singing the latest Coster favourites *'E dunno where 'e are'*, *'Take it in boys'* and *'The rickety, rackety crew.'*

Just a month later, in March 1892, Charles Kay looks set to try his musical comedy out on the London stage, as announced in *The East & South Devon Advertiser*. In a report on Variety Entertainment at the Mechanics Institute, it states that 'the building was crowded (said to be the largest of the season) by an audience who had, no doubt, braved the wind and weather, as Mr. C B Kay's appearance at the entertainment was to be his last local one, prior to his going to London to seek his fortune on the music hall stage. That popular young vocalist's songs were therefore looked upon as the feature of the evening, and his singing brought down the house.

'His first song was, *'You'll never see daylight again'* and in response to the determined encore with which it was received, Mr. Kay obliged with an extremely funny song *'That nose,'* which also drew forth roars of laughter and hearty applause. Mr. Kay was also very good in the burlesque duet *'The Sisters Frilling'* in which he was joined by Mr. Hambly, but his best effort was his rendering of a well-written parody on *'Ta-ra-ra-boom-de-ay'*. This song was looked forward to all the evening, and the recall was a most enthusiastic one. Mr. Kay of course willingly acceded to the wish of his admirers, and sang one or two more verses in which he introduced a much appreciated local hit concerning the recent police hoax.'

In a Stray Notes column by *'Rambler'* in the same issue of the newspaper, it stated that 'Mr. C B Kay, who made his debut as a comic vocalist at St. James's Hall, Plymouth, has decided to seek his

STRAY NOTES

BY "RAMBLER"

Mr. C. B. Kay, who made his debut as a comic vocalist at St. James's Hall, Plymouth, has decided to seek his fortune on the London music hall stage and by the time these lines are being printed the popular singer will probably have made a start on what all his friends will be the road to success. He has amused us with is excellent vocalisation, and various local "hits," why should he not prove himself capable of amusing London audiences?

East and South Devon Advertiser, 10th March, 1892. Image © The British Library Board. All rights reserved. Included with permission of the British Newspaper Archive. (www.britishnewspaperarchiveco,uk)

fortune on the London Music Hall stage, and by the time these lines are printed the popular singer will probably have made a start on what all his friends hope will be the road to success. He has amused us with his excellent vocalisation and various local hits, why should he not prove himself capable of amusing London audiences?

'It is a bold stroke for Mr. Kay to make, as anyone with knowledge of the metropolitan music halls would know; and the odds are against him are very great, but this should not deter him. I hope Mr. Kay's career will be brilliant and, in this wish, I know many will join me.'

Back performing in Newton

How successful Charles Kay's initial foray into the London stage actually was is difficult to ascertain as no newspaper or other references to him could be found at this time, but he is definitely back in Newton, Devon, by December 1892 and due to appear at a Smoking Concert at the Mid-Devon Constitutional Club. However, it was stated that Mr. C B Kay would be unable to sing, as expected, owing to a severe attack of neuralgia.

Nevertheless, he is soon organizing a successful variety entertainment at the Alexandra Hall in aid of the Newton Football Club. In a programme arranged by C B Kay that played to a house packed end-to-end at an early hour it was reported in *The East and South Devon Advertiser*, 25th February, that for Charles Kay's own act he came on stage 'in a most extravagant make-up' and sang *'Once more I sent the needful 18 stamps,'* which vastly pleased the house and in response to an encore sang *'Phew: them golden kippers,'* a song of his which always goes well.'

Entertainment at the Alexandra Hall in Aid of the Newton Football Club

A highly successful variety entertainment was held at the above Hall on Thursday last, the house being packed from end to end at an early hour. The programme, which was arranged by Mr. C B Kay commenced with a well-executed piano solo, 'Babylonia,' by Mr S R Curtis, musical director, who throughout the performance accompanied in his best style.

The East and South Devon Advertiser, Saturday 25th February, 1893. Image © The British Library Board. All rights reserved. Included with permission of the British Newspaper Archive (*www.britishnewspaperarchive.co.uk*)

Later in the programme, Charles Kay appeared again, clad this time as an aged Coster and sang Chevalier's masterpiece, *'My old Dutch'*, a most beautiful and pathetic song to which the audience listened with

Kay appeared as an aged Coster to sing Chevalier's masterpiece 'My old Dutch'

rapt attention. In part two of the programme, in a rustic scene, Miss Lilla Hosking – looking very sweet in her sun bonnet – and Mr. C B Kay performed *'Cicely Sweet.'*

During part three, C B Kay came back on with a black eye, strips of sticking plaster and a bedraggled suit of clothes and gave *'The man who **didn't** break the bank at Monte Carlo'*. It was reported that 'this fairly fetched the audience. Mr. Kay's sly hints at 'Rats' and 'Letters to the *Daily Mercury*' evidently being, in common parlance, 'twigged.' It was said that Mr. C B Kay stage managed the evening most effectively.'

While Charles Kay was widely lauded for his excellent comic singing voice and characterizations, it was perhaps something of a surprise to see a reference to him in the *East and South Devon Advertiser* on the 25th March 1893, that reported that: 'Mr. C B Kay is suffering from a very bad relaxed throat and will be unable to sing anymore this season. This is most unfortunate as he was engaged by Mrs. Splatt, Mayoress of Torquay, to fill the principal comedy part in a new opera shortly to be produced by her at Torquay and Plymouth.

In early July 1893, C B Kay and A W Dixon put on a couple of concerts at the Alexandra Hall, Newton, to contribute to the fund being raised for the relief of suffers from the disaster to the ironclad 'HMS Victoria,' the lead ship in her class of two battleships of the Royal Navy that sank on 22nd June 1893, after colliding with HMS Camperdown near Tripoli, Lebanon, during manoeuvers, killing 358 crew members, including the commander of the British Mediterranean Fleet, Vice-Admiral Sir George Tryon. Two excellent concert programmes were arranged for the fund, attended by a large and appreciative audience. The humorous element of the concerts was highly appreciated by the audience.

Mr. C B Kay won great success in his three songs. His first song *'Juh-Jah,'* the latest London success, received a unanimous recall, as also did *'The Rowdy-Dowdy boys.'* His other effort was *'The Seventh Royal Fusiliers, or a story of Inkerman,'* in which he was assisted by Masters J Hosking and C Hobbs. Owing to the public spirit and energy of Messrs. C B Kay and A W Dixon, Newton was able to contribute to the fund to raise money for the relief of the sufferers of the disaster.

A Ladies Night at the Newton Constitutional Club in October 1893 has Mr. Kay gaining an encore for each of his songs, *'My Fairy Mary Green,'* and a parody on *'Daisy Bell.'*

In something very different to his usual comic performances the *East and South Devon Advertiser* wrote in November 1893 of a dramatic performance at Newton, when the recently formed

Newton Constitutional Club Dramatic Society made its second public performance. It was the general opinion of the audience that the entertainment was one of the best ever given in the Club, and all the officials were to be congratulated on the success which had attended their efforts. Mr. C B Kay was the Society's Acting manager for the performance.

The following month, the *East and South Devon Advertiser* paper of 8th December makes mention of a crowded audience attending the 'Ladies night' at the Constitutional Club on the previous Friday evening. Mr. C B Kay's singing was heartily appreciated. His three songs were all encored, prime favourites being *'Gladdy's baby boy,'* *'Ladidily-umti-ay,'* and *'Little Alabaster coon.'*

The following week, on 16th December, the same newspaper reports on a social, again held at the Newton Constitutional Club, which attracted a large audience. Mr. C B Kay and Mr. W J Colwill's comic songs were well received, Mr. Kay's new song *'Pop went the weazel,'* bringing the house down. In response to the encore he sang a parody on *'Daisy Bell,'* introducing a verse about a recent encounter between ladies at Teignmouth. It was twice re-demanded. He also sang a parody on *'Daddy wouldn't buy me a bow wow.'*

In the same issue of the newspaper, a second report is on a Newton Football Club Benefit Concert given in the Alexandra Hall, by the Newton Variety Company, assisted by a few friends. Mr. C B Kay sang *'The Pretty Little Maiden's Sea Trip,'* and for the inevitable encore sang *'Linger Longer Loo.'* In the second part he gave *'Pop goes the weasel,'* and in reply to the encore *'Daisy*

Bell,' in which he introduced a verse relating the adventures of a local tradesman who recently dropped out of sight. Mr. Kay acted as manager and director of the concert, which was deemed a great success.

In March 1894, C B Kay appears in his one-act musical farce at the Newton Constitutional Club entitled *'The Money Lender.'* The cast was made-up of Ebeneezer Skinflint (of Goldwell Park, a millionaire) played by Mr. R J Rutland; Charles Skinflint (his son) played by Mr. C B Kay; Lord Hardup (an impecunious nobleman) played by Mr. R W Williams; Rosabella Hardup (his daughter) played by Mr. W H Pinsent; The Hon, Tom Oofless (a needy lordling) played by Mr. J H Wills; and Jeames (Skinflint's slave) played by Mr. J E Tuplin.

The part of Ebeneezer Skinflint was well taken by Mr. Rutland, who made an excellent old gentleman, and Mr. Kay capitally portrayed his gay son Charles. All the other characters had very little to do. Charles Skinflint sang *'The Bank that broke the man at Monte Carlo,'* and *'I'm the man that buried Tar-ra-ra-boom-de-ay.'*

Another highly successful concert took place at the Newton Constitutional Club in April 1894, where Mr. Kay – although evidently indisposed and looking rather done up after his heavy football tour, was very successful in *'At Trinity Church I met my doom,'* and as an encore gave *'Halfpast nine,'* the audience joining heartily in the chorus. Kay's second effort *'E's found out where 'e 'are'* was a huge success and as an encore gave *'Dolly on the ditties.'*

An amusing character comedian

Charles Kay is still performing at various local events in Newton throughout 1894, 1895 and 1896; newspaper reports during this time first show him at a Newton Conservative Club Concert in October 1894, where he is listed in the performances as singing comic songs entitled *'Oom pah'* and *'Me and 'er'*.

This was followed the next week when he was on stage at the Alexandra Hall, Newton, for a Grand Concert in which, as the amusing character comedian with his highly amusing songs, sang *'Oom-Pah'* and then *'Little alabaster coon.'*

Just a month later he is amongst the performers in a Social at *'Ye Courtenay'* Lodge in connection with the RAOB. This was held at the Newfoundland Hotel. During the evening Bros. C B Kay sang *'Nurse the royal coon,'* which was encored.

Moving into 1895, a capital concert is given in the schoolroom at Littlehampton

A caricature of Charles Kay in his 'masher' costume, the 1890 period name for what was previously known a few years earlier as a dandy.

in aid of the fund for the summer outing of the choir. In Part One of the programme the audience were thoroughly awakened when Mr. C B Kay in a 'masher' costume sang *'All in a romp,'* and in response to an undeniable encore, he re-appeared in *'Hi diddly up to,'* which was given in characteristic humor and proved exceedingly funny. Masher trousers were tight and of equal width at the knee and ankle, and came with tightly cinged waists, flared frock coats, high collars, with a large bow at the neck.

Mr. Kay came on later in a clerical dress, plus a wig, and gave the song *'Pinky Ponky Poo'* in imitable style, a vociferous encore being bestowed, to which he responded with *'Oompah,'* which caught on with the audience vigorously applauding him at the conclusion.

In between his concert appearances he also found time to organize an ice hockey match. With severe low temperatures and frozen lakes in Devon during February 1895, it was reported in the *Western Morning News* that an exciting ice hockey match had taken place on Stover Lake (now part of the 114 acre Stover Country Park, Newton Abbot) between a Dawlish team and a team of Torquay gentlemen, captained by Mr. C B Kay. It was stated that Stover Lake was crowded with several hundred skaters, the weather was glorious and the ice, which was said to be 8-9 inches thick, was in perfect condition. Some fast play by both sides took place, with Mr. Kay's team eventually winning by nine goals to eight – of which six were scored by Mr. Kay.

Just a few weeks later another report, this time in the *East and South Devon Advertiser*, talks of an ice hockey tournament at Stover Park during the severe weather which produced some of the finest skating in Devon – in fact, the whole West of Engaland. Over 300 people attended, on ice said to be in places some 14 inches thick. The Newton Hockey team, organised and captained by C B Kay, won seven out of the eight matches placed. Mr. Kay, with a total of 25 goals, was the principal scorer.

In March of that year, at a well-attended (very few seats being empty) concert held in the Public Rooms at Newton, Mr. Kay introduced his new stuttering song, *'Ga-Ga-Good Bye,'* which particularly pleased the critics at the back of the room, and for the encore he gave that excellent example of modern humour song, *'The Tin Gee Gee.'*

In his second song, *'Perhaps, per'ps not,'* Mr Kay introduced the following topical verse:

'All good people at the Workhouse now lead a happy life
　　　Perhaps, per'ps
The Guardians never quarrel and there's never any strife
　　　Perhaps, per,ps
Of nasty, happy, jumping things there's never any specks
The children walk out daily in brand new suits of checks
And get some heathers, dare to say they never wash their necks
　　　Perhaps, per,ps not

In response to the encore Kay sang his popular song *'Pinky Ponky Poo.'*

Later, in August 1895, there was a concert in the Parish Room at Lustleigh, a village nestled in the Wrey Valley. Mr. C B Kay appeared in his best style singing *'Louisiana Lou,'* his stuttering song, *'Ga-ga- good-bye,'* followed by *'Me and 'er,'* and *'Jimmy on the Clute,'* for each of which he received vociferous encores.

Also in 1895 he is again on stage at a concert organised by the Royal Antediluvian Order of Buffaloes where 'the presence of Bro.

C B Kay, in character, on the platform was a signal in itself for an outburst of applause. *'The sweetest flower dies,'* a new song, Bro. Kay sang with all his well-known characteristic portrayal, and with so much consummate success, that the demand for a hearty encore was inevitable. Bro. Kay kindly responded with *'Me and 'er,'* and again earned new laurels.

It was noted that after dinner Bro. Kay sang in character (a splendid get up) *'In her own backyard,'* as well as an entirely new song, which took immediately. Encore upon encore followed, and Bro. Kay complied, singing another of his comic songs, *'Pinky, Ponky, Poo,'* equally bright and sparkling.

Back on the stage in October 1895, in a Ye Courtenay Lodge concert again held at the RAOB Newfoundland Hall, a large audience of brothers and friends saw the MC for the evening, Mr. C B Kay attend in an extravagant Bloomer costume (a short jacket, a skirt extending below the knee, and loose 'Turkish' trousers, gathered at the ankles) of a starling hue, and causing roars of laughter by his singing of *'It hurts'*. In response, he gave *'Beer, glorious beer.'*

The last item on the programme was also furnished by Mr. Kay who, still dressed in his Bloomer costume, sang *'Salute my bicycle'* and for the recall sang *'She wanted something to play with'* in which he introduced some 'local' verses.

At the end of November 1895, the Dawlish Constitutional Club held its opening concert of the season. The room was crowded to excess, with Mr. C B Kay the popular comic, being specially engaged for the occasion. It was said that the audience was not satisfied until he had contributed some eight songs:

'Salute my bicycle'

'He takes me up in the gallery'

'Can't stop'

' It hurts'

'The little ones at home'

'Dark blue eyes'

'Ga-ga, good bye (his hilarious stuttering song)'

'She wanted something to play with.'

This last song, with Kay's own local allusions, was very acceptable.

In December 1895, the Concert Room at the Newton Liberal Club was said to have been filled to an uncomfortable extent for the occasion of the first 'Ladies Night' of the season. Mr. C B Kay, again attired in a hybrid Bloomer costume, introduced a couple of new songs, *'Poor old Jones'* and *'The beautiful story of love'*.

At the end of January 1896 Charles Kay is among the performers at a Grand Evening Concert at the Mid-Devon Constitutional Club in which the large hall and adjoin billiard room were crowded to their utmost capacity and many were unable to obtain seats. The *East and South Devon Advertiser* of 1st February 1896 reported that 'Mr. C B Kay was prominent with *'The gay tom-tit'* from *'The artist's model,'* which is now on the boards in London, followed by *'It is not true'* and *'Can't stop.'* On each occasion Mr. Kay met with loud encore. One of his encore songs *'Faces'* being distinctly funny and causing great merriment.'

Later in February, C B Kay is performing in a benefits concert at the Alexandra Hall in Newton Abbot in aid of the Great Western

Railway Servants', Widows' and Orphans' Fund. In the first part of the concert Mr. Kay introduced a new patriotic song *'What is our own we'll hold.'* The second part of the concert was devoted to the production of a burlesque entitled *'An altogether moral Trilby,'* written by Mr. Kay at short notice. The newspaper report said that 'As a writer of impromptu verses to comic songs Mr. Kay has frequently scored successes, but this was his first essay at playwriting. It was not surprising therefore, that the work bore the stamp of the amateur, though there is sufficient promise in it to warrant the author courting the muses again.'

However, at the beginning of November 1896 he leaves all of Newton Abbott wondering, the *East & South Devon Advertiser* reporting that that they had heard on good authority that Mr. C B Kay had sailed for South Africa.

Serious charges

It was in late November 1896 that something approaching a sensation started to run through Newton Abbot, when rumors started to spread that Mr. Charles Beachy Kay, the well-known comic singer, had been apprehended in St John's Wood, London, by a Detective Cook, where he was charged with abduction of a girl under the age of 17 and 'taking an unmarried girl out of the possession and against the will of her father with the intention to carnally know her.'

The *East and South Devon Advertiser* on Saturday 21st November commented that 'As an entertainer and vocalist Mr. Kay had been in such constant request in South Devon during the past five years, and had appeared so frequently at all the towns and villages in the district, that he was familiar to everyone.'

It added that he was also well-known on the football fields, having played as a forward for Newton, Torquay Athletic, Exeter and other towns. As a cricketer he had assisted Dawlish, Newton, South Devon and Starcross clubs, and was the moving spirit of the Newton Hockey Club.

In outlining the charges, the newspaper went on to say that 'Several years ago Mr. Kay was married to a young lady of prepossessing appearance, and had since been living with his wife and family at Newton on his private income. There were four children of the marriage. However, in the early part of the summer, Mr. Kay had left Newton to reside at Dawlish, his wife and family remaining in Newton. Then, about three weeks ago it was announced that Mr. Kay had left England for Johannesburg, South Africa, 'where he had no appointment.'

'Within the same week a warrant was issued at Teignmouth for his arrest on the application of Mr. Henry Samuel Martin, a gentleman of independent means of Bishopsteignton, who charged him with abducting his daughter, Carrie Louise Martin, aged 17.' The report went on to say that the efforts of the police to find Mr. Kay were for some days very fruitless, but on the Friday last the Chief Constable of Devon had received information that Mr. Kay had been arrested in London, and on the same day was handed over to a Detective Cook, of Exeter, by the Metropolitan Police, having been discovered living at St John's Wood Road – a London neighbourhood with a low reputation – with Miss Martin as Mr. and Mrs. Beechcroft. He was subsequently brought to Exeter and detained in custody over Sunday.

On the Monday morning the case came up for an initial hearing at Teignmouth Police Court. It was said that the news of his hearing had spread as rapidly as news of Mr. Kay's character usually did and as the defendant walked through the streets most of the town were on the lookout for him. He was then quickly recognised, dressed in a dark suit, with black overcoat, tan gloves, and carrying a walking stick with a silver knob. The Town Hall was crowded in every part, all the forms being fully occupied and many having to stand.

SPECIAL EDITION

TO-DAY'S WIRES

GIRL OF 17

ALLEGED ABDUCTION BY A MAN OF INDEPENDENT MEANS

At Teignmouth, to-day, Charles Beachy Kay, of Newton Abbot, was charged with abducting Carrie Louise Martin, aged 17, of Bishop Steignton. Accused, who is of independent means, was apprehended.

Extract from the Daily Mail of 16th November 1896. Image © The British Library Board. All rights reserved. Included with permission of the British Newspaper Archive (www.britishnewspaperarchive.co.uk)

After a licensing case was disposed of the Clerk of the Court called on Mr. Kay. It was recorded that he stepped into the dock with a jaunty air and, whilst the case was being heard leant back against the rail of the dock, his left foot resting on the low dock rail in front. After listening to the evidence and after much discussion about sureties, the Bench granted bail for the defendant himself in £500, and two other sureties of £250 each, the case was adjourned, with the defendant asked to return to Court on the Monday next at eleven o'clock.

The following Monday Teignmouth Police Court was again crowded in every part when the adjourned case against Mr. Kay came up for the second hearing. The audience this time included many tradesmen of the town, several persons from Newton who were well acquainted with the prisoner, and a good sprinkling of the fair sex. Two of the prosecutor's four daughters sat on a bench near the top end of the court.

After a fairly lengthy hearing, largely revolving around whether the girl's father knew that the defendant and the girl had been sleeping together, and then much discussion by witnesses on how old they thought the girl was, the Bench retired, and after a few minutes deliberation returned. The Bench unanimously agreed that there was sufficient evidence to go before a jury and that Mr. Kay would have to take trial at the next Assizes. Again, bail was granted in the total sureties of £1,000.

At this second court hearing, Detective Cook said the girl had the appearance of a 20-year old, and that the two of them had been living together in London as a Mr. and Mrs. Beachcroft. Defending, Mr. Beal, of Exeter, argued that the girl was prematurely aged in appearance and

PETITE, BUT PRETTY
ALLEGED ABDUCTION OF A GIRL OF SEVENTEEN

At Teignmouth to-day, Charles Beachy Kay, a married man with a wife and three children, living in Newton Abbot, was charged on remand with abducting Carrie Louise Martin, aged 17, daughter of of a jeweller at Bishop Steignton. Accused was well dressed and bore himself up

Daily Mail, 23rd November 1896.

that the accused thought she was much older than her years. Giving evidence, the girl said that she had not been abducted, but had accompanied Kay at her own free will. Indeed, said Mr. Beal, she had stated that she would not go back to her father's home at any price.

It was reported during the hearing that Kay was a 'gentleman of independent means', but that he 'already' had connections with the London theatre stage as a comedian. One newspaper report stated that the accused appeared in the dock 'fashionably dressed', while the *Hull Daily Mail* noted that 'the accused was well dressed, and bore himself with confidence.' The newspaper also added that the girl, 'who was also smartly dressed, was petite, but pretty.' Reports of the case widely appeared in newspapers throughout England.

During the hearing the girl's father, Henry Samuel Martin, said the girl had received presents from Kay, including a bicycle, and that he himself had borrowed money from him. His daughter had frequently slept away from home, but always told him that she was staying with a married friend (she was, it was Charles Kay). He also said that he knew the prisoner was married, but considered him honorable. The Bench determined there was a case for a jury, with Kay again being remanded by the court on bail in the sum of £1,000 (in excess of £60,000 in the 21st century).

At the later Assizes trial, Kay told the court that his wife had now issued divorce proceedings and that when this went through he would be able to marry the girl. The court prosecutor then stated that as both the police officer and the girl's father had stated that the girl looked over 20, she herself had stated that she went with him of her own free will, and that Kay had now promised to marry her, they would abstain from offering any prosecution evidence. He was then discharged.

The couple continued living in London at that time under his new adopted name, Charles Beachy Kay Beachcroft – perhaps strangely incorporating his first wife's maiden name (Beachy) as part of his new name.

His wife did indeed subsequently petition for divorce in consequence of her husband's cruelty and adultery, claiming that he had bruised and beaten her on a number of occasions, had tightly squeezed her neck and also injured her back by pushing her out of bed – for which she needed medical treatment from a Dr Grimbly. She also claimed that he regularly stayed out late and refused to cohabit with her.

Subsequently, she discovered that Kay had been cohabiting with Carrie Martin at the Farley Hotel, Union Street, Plymouth, in April 1896 and had been committing adultery with her from late 1895 when the girl was only 16. When she accused him of adultery, he had run off to London with the girl. His wife was subsequently granted a decree Nisi in August 1897, with costs, and given custody of their children. Kay was ordered to pay a total of £3.00 per week for the maintenance of his four children.

Rose Kay later re-married and emigrated to Cape Town, South Africa, in 1898 with her two youngest children, Florence Beachy Kay and Henry Aubrey Kay. Florence eventually married a Dennis

Burton Kelly in South Africa while, in World War I, Aubrey enlisted in the South African Overseas Expeditionary Force, a volunteer force under British operational command that had been formed by the South African Government in 1915 as its contribution to the British war effort.

The two youngest of Charles and Rose Kay's children remained in England and in the 1901 census were living with their grandmother, Bessie Kay Heaton, at 133 West Cliff, Dawlish.

Meanwhile, following this divorce, Charles Beachy Kay Beachcroft, by now temporarily living back in Devon at the London Hotel, Exeter, did go on and marry Carrie Martin. This took place in the Strand, London, Registry District, on 19th October 1897. It was stated in the marriage document that she had been born in Cheltenham in 1879. After the ceremony Mr. and Mrs. Kay Beachcroft are said to have entertained a large party at the Adelphi Hotel.

It is perhaps ironic that, given his prosecution for abduction of a young girl, and his earlier court appearance for trespassing on the railway, that before the decree is granted he is recorded as appearing in a charity event in the Alexandra Hall in February 1896 in aid of the Great Western Railways Servants, Widows and Orphan's Fund. Charles Kay played Svengali in a performance of 'An altogether moral Trilby'. Performances were given in the

MR C. B. KAY AND HIS MEDICAL ATTENDANT

———

Charles Beachy Kay Beachcroft of Newton Abbot, was summoned, but did not appear at the Newton Abbot County Court yesterday to answer a claim by Richard Henry Grimbly, surgeon, of Newton, for £7. 13s, due for medical attendance. Mr Woollcombe (Baker, Watts, Alsop, and Woollcombe) appeared for the plaintiff, and asked for an order of payment forthwith. He did not know how defendant lived

From the Devon and Exeter Gazette, September 18th, 1897. Image © The British Library Board. All rights reserved. Included with permission of the British Newspaper Archive (www.britishnewspaperarchive.co.uk)

afternoon and evening, both preceded by a concert in which Kay sang as a humorous vocalist.

In early 1898, Charles Beachy Kay Beachcroft, now permanently living back in Devon with his new wife and already one child – Henry George Beachcroft – is once again being summoned to appear at Newton Abbot Count Court, this time to answer a claim by Dr. Richard Henry Grimbly, a surgeon, in the sum of £7.13 due for medical attendance to his former wife. He did not appear in court and the plaintiff said that the last time he had heard from Kay he was touring in a theatrical company in London. The defendant's mother, who was in court, said her son was rather erratic, but that the money would be paid.

In April 1899 Charles Beachy Kay Beachcroft is reported as being back in a court, but this time claiming money, £34.18s.3d, from a Mr. T Hills, a London bookmaker, for money due on an account. It was said that Beachcroft had a habit of betting with the defendant and had in this case placed thirty-two shillings through a Mr. Nicholls on an each-way bet on three horses running in the Liverpool Cup.

He later received a telegram from the bookmaker's brother, a clerk in the business, saying he had won £34.18s.3d. However, he had never been paid, as the bookmaker refused to pay out the money, claiming in turn, that as Mr. Nicholls actually owed him money he would not pay out any winnings. The court case was adjourned for evidence of the bet, the telegram and the winnings to be produced. No record of the subsequent finding has yet been found.

Landlord and sporting host

A month or so later in the January of 1898, Charles Beachcroft is now in the process of borrowing £3,000 to purchase the lease, stock, furniture and effects of the Royal Hotel, Dawlish, with him becoming the landlord and the licensed victualler. The Hotel originally descended from the Dawlish Public Rooms and at one time was owned by the Dean of York. It first appeared under the name of the Royal Hotel in 1867, one of the new owner/occupiers being a William Hatcher. As can be seen from the advertisement, the hotel was regarded as one of the best in Dawlish and offered sea views, a smoking lounge, billiards room, a public library, fine accommodation and stabling.

The "Gazette

HOTEL LIST
—

THE HOUSES TO STAY AT

DAWLISH
ROYAL HOTEL
THE BEST FAMILY HOTEL

Uninterrupted Sea View. Close to G.W.R. Station. New Smoking Lounge. Billiard Room. Hot and Cold Baths. Public Library. Fine accommodation for Tourists And Cyclists. Table d'Hote every Evening At Separate Tables. Good Stabling.

C.B.K. BEACHCROFT, Manager

Taken from an advert in The Devon and Exeter Gazette, October 1, 1898.
Image © The British Library Board. All rights reserved. Included with permission of the British Newspaper Archive (www. britishnewspaperarchive.co.uk)

At around the same time as this purchase, Beachcroft was once again beginning to make various and more frequent performances at public events and on the local stage, becoming even more well known around the West Country and further afield as something of an excellent amateur singer, humourist and entertainer.

In June 1898, now more commonly known in the sporting world as C B K Beachcroft, he is reported as giving his fourth and final smoking concert at the Royal Hotel Assembly Rooms on Saturday 16th June, under the patronage of the combined Exeter Cycling Club. There was a large audience and each artist received rounds of applause. Mr. Beachcroft contributed to the entertainment and 'great credit was due to him for his able management of the evening.'

In September that same year, as landlord of the Royal Hotel, he donates a handsome and valuable silver cup to the H (Dawlish) Company 1st R.V. to be shot for by the members at their next prize shooting meeting. Two months later, members of the Company held their annual dinner at the Royal Hotel. A large turnout was hosted by Beachcroft who is said to have served up an excellent dinner.

Becoming the landlord of the Royal Hotel, together with his interest in shooting, also seems to have spurred Charles Beachcroft's gambling and wager fervour, with him now starting to regularly organise a variety of sporting gaming events for money or sweepstakes.

Indeed, in the following month, October 1898, C B K Beachcroft is reported in the local newspaper as organising a rabbit coursing event in Dawlish. It was noted that 'the day was somewhat marred by poor weather, although good running was encountered by those attending. Mr. Beachcroft's dog 'Sporto' proved to be the fastest dog in the field.' He also raced his dog 'Bob'. After the coursing, dinner was held at the Royal Hotel.

In January 1899, C B K Beachcroft is now arranging for a party of sportsmen to meet on the Dawlish racecourse to try and assess the quality of each of their dogs. The event was said to be all that could be desired, although the supply of rabbits was limited. The results included Mr. Beachcroft's dog 'Buddy' beating Mr. Singleton's dog 'Fuzzy' in the final. Mr. Beachcroft's dog 'Sporto' also beat Mr. Rowell's dog 'Rough'. After the coursing all the sportsmen again left for dinner at the Royal Hotel.

That same month Beachcroft is summoned to attend the Newton County Court as the joint defendant in a case brought by the National Telephone Company for non-payment of £10.15s, one year's rent in advance for the hire of a telephonic instrument used at the Royal Hotel. The Court found in favour of the National Telephone Company but Beachcroft & Co, named as the present tenant of the hotel was acquitted as he was only the tenant.

A few weeks later a party of sportsmen from Exeter, Teignmouth, Torquay and Dawlish met for lunch at Beachcroft's Royal Hotel, after which they proceeded to the rugby football club field and race course to enjoy themselves. The first events on the programme were three pigeon shooting contests for sweepstakes of 10s, 15s, and 20s respectively. It was said that in each competition 'much spirit and good marksmanship was enjoyed'. All these shooting sweepstakes were won by C B K Beachcroft (shooting an incredible 20 pigeons out of 20 over the three competitions). Following the pigeon shoot, the sportsmen enjoyed some very good rabbit coursing. Mr. Beachcroft's 'Patrick' beat Mr. Piles 'Monte Carlo'. Beachcroft also had wins with his dogs 'Buddy' and 'Sporto'.

Then in April 1899, Beachcroft is noted as attending the Easter Devon Pigeon Shoot organised by Mr. Ball of the Albert Hotel,

Dawlish. This event was attended by sportsmen from all over Devon. First prize was a pen of fat lambs valued at £10. 10s, and for which there were ten competitors. Shooting for this prize was said to be the best ever seen. Unfortunately, the prize was not settled as the competition ran out of pigeons – leaving six competitors each of whom had shot all ten of their birds. Beachcroft was one of these remaining six. He certainly seems to have been a prestigious shot.

Among Charles Beachcroft's other abilities he was certainly able to prove that he was a keen and good swimmer. In June 1899 he appears in several newspaper reports relating to a sad bathing fatality in which a Mr. Henry Brown from London had gone to Coryton Gentleman's Bathing Cove in Dawlish to take a bath, upon which he at once swam out to sea. Suddenly he was seen to throw up his arms and cry for help. In the water at this time were Mr. Beachcroft and Mr. Jones and they at once went to the man's aid. Unfortunately Brown was gradually carried out further by the current and they were unable to reach him. At this time Mr. Jones himself became exhausted and it was with great difficulty that he was eventually supported by Mr. Beachcroft back to the shore. The body of Mr. Brown was later recovered from the sea. A subsequent inquest returned a verdict of 'Accidental drowning.' It was later announced that Kay had been presented with The Royal Humane Society Medal for Lifesaving.

In another report, of a Lawn Tennis Tournament held at Dawlish, Mr. C B Kay competed with Mr. S Waters in the gentlemen's doubles, narrowly losing to their opponents.

A later report from 1899 sees Beachcroft visiting Paris with the members of the Devon County Wanderers cricket team, and noting that the team had been undefeated in all the matches they had played, while *The Western Times* of September 19th 1899 notes that Beachcroft was the second highest scorer in a match between Dawlish and Sheldon.

An all-round sporting gentleman

By the early 1900s there are many local reports that state that Charles Beachey Kay Beachcroft, or now simply C B K Beachcroft, was a frequent visitor to Barnstable as a well-known rugby footballer, as well as a cricketer and hockey player. He is also referred to as an old Newton College boy and played Rugby for Dawlish, Torquay and Newton Abbot, and also made a lot of big scores at cricket playing for Newton Blues, South Devon and Exeter.

He was also a member of the newly formed Devon County Hockey Association and on January 16th 1902 was selected to play as a forward for Devon against Dorset, at Poole. At the annual meeting of the Hockey Association held at the Bude Hotel Exeter in October 1902 Mr. Beachcroft, now the Hon. Secretary, stated that nine matches had been played during the season – six won and three lost. Amongst the motions presented it was agreed that all members that had accrued their caps by playing in three county matches should pay for the caps – and for their shirts.

Around the same time, *Devon and Exeter Gazette* states that the Hockey Club had achieved a promising start to the season with an easy win in the first of an attractive list of fixtures. The Exeter forwards, who included Eyre, Preston Thomas and Beachcroft – three of the County forwards – had carried all before them. It was Beachcroft that opened the scoring.

Also taking place in October was a hockey match between Exeter and Exeter Reserves, won easily by six goals to one, of which Beachcroft had scored three for Exeter. He is also still playing cricket, as reported in the *East & South Devon Advertiser* of 4th October where it was noted that Beachcroft completed his 1,000 runs for the season during a game in which he played for Mr.Rendell's XI against Teignmouth, Beachcroft's team winning by 133 runs to 45.

In November 1902, the Exeter hockey team played Ottery St. Mary. It was said that 'the grass was too long and the turf heavy.' Nevertheless, Exeter soon pressed and Beachcroft, playing centre, 'ran through and scored easily, scoring again before half-time'. He scored again in the second half for Exeter to win 6-2.

Later in the month, Exeter is shown as playing against an Ashbury hockey team. Exeter won 30-nil with great ease. Beachcroft was said to have had an excellent day, scoring 5 of the winning goals.

December then sees Mr. C B Kay's hockey team giving an exhibition of roller skating against a team organized by Mr. Mead at the Congress Hall. Roller skating was still a relatively new sport in England in the early 1900s and was using skates developed in the later part of the 1800s which incorporated ball bearings in skate wheels to reduce friction and increase speed, as well as toe stops enabling the skater to stop promptly when the skate was tipped – the forerunners of today's modern roller skates.

Then, early in 1903 the Exeter hockey team played Mr. Cheeseworth's XI. Although Exeter fielded a weak team they were still able to win easily by eight goals to three. Beachcroft scored four of the goals. February 1903 also sees a hockey match arranged between Dawlish and a team organised by Mr. Beachcroft, won easily by the Beachcroft's.

Apart from his busy activities as hockey secretary and key player, C B K Beachcroft now becomes involved in a new sport – ping-pong. Indeed, he is instrumental in bringing this new game to Devon. The media in January 1902 had stated that ping-pong was 'a game played by gentlemen on the sacred surfaces of the dinner table. When the silverware and the table cloth were removed from the table, and the ladies had withdrawn, then the process of digestion could begin by hitting a small celluloid ball across a net with a pair of parchment 'battledoors'. This is the game of table tennis, better known as ping-pong'.

Within a couple of months Beachcroft has become the Secretary of the newly formed Exeter Ping-Pong Association, and at the forefront of introducing the sport to Devon. By early April 1902 he is organising a ping-pong match between his own side and a side put together by a Mr. Horrell. Beachcroft went on to beat his opponents in both the singles and doubles. He certainly seems adapt at any sport involving a ball.

Such was his success, that by the middle of May 1902, the Exeter Ping-Pong Association is able to announce their 10th consecutive victory, with a total of 92 points and 11 games, while a local store announces a new stock of ping-pong sets from just 1s. Another store carries an advert for 'Ladies Ping-Pong Corsets.'

May 1902 also sees large crowds attending the Trades Exhibition at the Victoria Hall, Exeter, where the Viennese Ladies Orchestra was a great attraction, while there was also a good deal of interest in a ping-pong tournament between teams captained by

Mr. J Webber and Mr. C B K Beachcroft.

PING-PONG

GRAND OPEN HANDICAP TOURNA-MENT for the Championship of the City and a Solid Silver Cup, value £3. Entries (fee 2s) close Saturday, April 26. 9 p.m.
C. B. K. BEACHCROFT Hon. Sec.

Advert in Devon & Exeter Gazette, April 25th, 1902. Image © The British Library Board. All rights reserved. Included with permission of the British Newspaper Archive (www.britishnewspaperarchive.co.uk)

Beachcroft can then be found placing an advert in the *Devon & Exeter Gazette* announcing a Grand Open Handicap Ping-Pong Tournament, the prize being a handsome solid silver cup worth £3.00. He also organises various ping-pong demonstration matches around the county. By June 1902 the Evening Telegraph is saying that 'the game of ping-pong is spreading like wildfire and 1902 will prove to be a veritable ping-ponger of a year.' A tournament in Manchester was to claim a spectator attendance of some 2,000 people.

However, the success and popularity of the game was not without its problems. The *British Medical Journal* of that year carried a report that the game was causing teno-synovitis – which hurts very much. The disease causes inflammation of the tendons connected with the muscles around the shin.

Another consequence of the growing interest in pin-pong was that by August 1902 local magistrates were deciding that the game came within the provisions of the Gaming Act of 1845, meaning proprietors of cafes and restaurants that had ping-pong tables amongst their attractions now had to take out a license. Many didn't and were prosecuted.

In February 1902, and again in 1903, Beachcroft is on the Committee of the Exeter Amateur Rowing Club and attending their annual dinners – and favoured the assembled company on both occasions with several of his concert songs. He also participated in the Rowing Club's opening day river trip in May 1902. This consisted of some 80 members and friends leaving the Port Royal boathouse in a steam launch heading for Starcross. The weather was said to be windy and showery, but cleared up beautifully later in the afternoon. High tea was taken at the Courtenay Arms, Starcross, at six o'clock, followed by a smoking concert, at which some capital songs were sung by Mr. C B K Beachcroft and others.

He also took part in February 1903 as a member, and entertainer, at the Second Annual Dinner of the Exonia Rifle Club, contributing to the harmony of the evening.

While Beachcroft is busily engaged as Hon. Secretary of both the hockey and ping-pong clubs, he is still finding time for playing cricket. He opens his 1902 cricket season as captain of a Dawlish team playing against his own Exeter Ping-Pong Association, for which of course he happens to be the Secretary. It is noted that he carries his bat throughout the Dawlish innings, scoring 48 runs, and then captured 5 of the opponent's wickets for just 5 runs.

There are other frequent references to his cricketing prowess. In September 1903, in the last match of the season he is noted as one of the highest scorers for Dawlish. The following month at the Dawlish Cricket Club annual meeting, Beachcroft is listed as the second highest scorer of the season with an average of 22.4 runs per innings.

The following year, in June 1904, he is noted as playing for Teignmouth against Newton College, while in September 1904 in a match between Dawlish and Dartmouth & Paington, it is noted that 'Mr. Beachcroft had the satisfaction of achieving 1,000 runs for the season.' In the last match for Exeter that season it is was stated that Ashford, Kneel and Beachcroft were the leading run scorers. Indeed, by now, Beachcroft is being referred to as the Dawlish W G Grace.

Other reports at the time say that he had played as opening batsman for Exeter Cricket Club, as well as turning out for Castle Carey Cricket Club and for Starcross (a small coastal parish on the Exe estuary between Exeter and Dawlish).

Sadly for the Dawlish Cricket Club – as well as the hockey, rugby and ping-pong associations – he leaves both the Club and Devon at the end of 1904 to once again try his hand at becoming a professional actor, comedian, and variety artist on the London and provincial stage, although there is still a sporting reference in the *Exeter and Plymouth Gazette* from this period which refers to C B K Beachcroft as being on the committee and attending the Annual Dinner of the Exeter Rowing Club.

Even after he has moved to London he is still to be found playing cricket. In June 1905, he is noted in the *Sporting Life* as playing cricket for Battersea against Brixton

In a much later clipping in *The Stage* Newspaper there is a reference to him as at one time being a former Devonshire County Cricketer, hockey club secretary, and as having a commission as a Lieutenant in the City of London Regiment, a Territorial Army Reserve regiment.

However, it was in 1900 that he undoubtedly achieved his greatest sporting success.

Gold medal winner in the 1900 Summer Olympics

In August 1900, at the Great Exposition and Paris Summer Olympic games, Charles Beachcroft (C B K Beachcroft) captained a Great Britain/England cricket team (essentially the Devon and Somerset Wanderers touring team) that beat a French team over two days to win an Olympic Gold medal – not that the team knew this at the time. Initially they had been awarded a silver medal and France a bronze medal for playing in a cricket competition as part of the Paris World Fair, an event so big that it was said to have been visited by nearly 50 million people. It was only some years later (in 1912) that these medals were upgraded by the Olympic Committee to gold and silver Olympic medals. It seems doubtful that he was ever aware of this, as there are no references to this ever being acknowledged or mentioned by him.

The 1900 Summer Olympics, better known today as the Games of the II Olympiad, was an international multi-sport event. No opening or closing ceremonies were held; competitions began on May 14 and ended on October 28. The Games were held as part of the 1900 Great Exposition or World Fair. Some 997 competitors took part in 19 different sports.

The cricket competition, in which France were originally scheduled to play matches against the Netherlands, Belgium and Great Britain was played at the Velodrome de Vincennes in Paris, a 20,000-seater cycle track. In the end, Belgium did not send their team, the Netherlands were unable to field a full team, and only the Great Britain/England versus France match actually took place. This was the only time that cricket had ended up becoming an

Olympic event, although it had been previously scheduled, but never played due to lack of entries, in the 1896 Games in Athens.

The Great Britain/England team was made up of Beachy Beachcroft (captain), Arthur Birkett, John Symes, Frederick Cuming, Montagu Toller, Alfred Bowerman, Alfred Powlesland, William Donne, Frederick Christian, George Buckley, Francis Burchell, Harry Corner. Although Great Britain were shown as playing a French team, the French side was mostly made-up of English expatriates living and working in Paris..

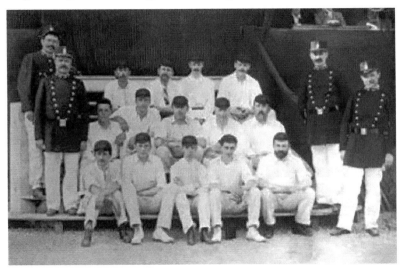

The Olympic gold medal winning team at the 1900 Summer Olympics in Paris. Charles Beachcroft is the third cricketer from the left in the middle row. Charles Beachcroft is the third cricketer from the left in the middle row.

One write-up of the match states that 'Great Britain batted first, and sent in the wonderfully named pair of Charles Beachy Kay Beachcroft (the captain) and Arthur Ernest Barrington Birkett. Beachcroft scored 21 runs in his first innings and 54 in the second before being run out.'

In both innings these scores were the second highest of the England batting. Other reports stated that in the second innings 'Beachcroft was again successful, reaching half-a-century. As for the French team, five consecutive members were to score ducks.

'Whatever chance France had of coming back into the match in the second innings had been ruled out by Beachy Beachcroft and Bowerman, who scored 54 and 59 respectively. Beachcroft declared the British innings closed at 145 for five, setting the French a target of 185 — a target definitely beyond them given their first innings performance was only 78 runs.'

The team's time in Paris was part of a two week tour and they had already completed five previous tours across the English Channel before travelling to France for the World Fair/Olympic cricket match. Following the game, the Devon and Somerset Wanderers played two further one-day cricket matches in France, winning them both.

As a postscript to the match it was reported that 'The victorious team's journey back to the hotel was eventful. The driver of one of the two coaches had become rather caught up in the day's events, had consumed far too much alcohol, and had to be driven back inside his own carriage. The other, apparently in a similarly excitable state, crashed his coach, causing minor injuries to some of the passengers.'

In the 1901 Census, Charles B K Beachcroft, occupation licensed victualler, and his wife Carrie are recorded as staying as visitors with Herbert Grantham, licensed victualler in Topsham, Devon.

Sad failure of Beachcroft's hotel ventures

The sporting achievements of Charles Beachey Kay Beachcroft do not seem to have had much successful influence on his business achievements however. A cutting from an October 4th 1901 edition of the *Western Times*, Devon, has Charles Beachcroft, the Licensed Victualler of the Royal Hotel, Dawlish – for which he had purchased the lease, furniture and fittings back in 1898 for £3,000 – appearing before Deputy Registrar J Dawes, at the Exeter Bankruptcy Court on 3rd October, later being declared bankrupt.

> ### A DAWLISH BANKRUPT
> ---
> At the Exeter Bankruptcy Court yesterday, before Deputy-Registrar, J. Daw, Charles Beachey Kay Beachcroft, Licensed Victualler, late of the Royal Hotel, Dawlish, attended for the purpose

Extract from the Western Times, October 4th 1901. Image © The British Library Board. All rights reserved. Included with permission of the British Newspaper Archive (www.britishnewspaperarchive.co.uk)

His liabilities at the time were said to be £52.13.2d and his assets as nil. Beachcroft attributed his failure to heavy rent and expenses and losses while in business. Indeed, he claimed to have worked at a loss during his whole period of trading at the Royal Hotel – not withstanding all the numerous successful sporting and charity dinners he arranged and held at the hotel. Beachcroft was represented in court by Mr. Crompton who, after the bankruptcy hearing was closed, announced he had lodged a scheme for settlement with the petitioning creditor, and at the next County Court, would be applying for the bankruptcy to be annulled.

However, it appears that Kay was already no longer living at the hotel, or indeed in Dawlish, at the time of the bankruptcy hearing. A local newspaper report in January 1901, noted that Mr. Chas.

Beachcroft, the proprietor of the Royal Hotel, Dawlish, until a few weeks since, had been presented with a silver mounted hunting crop, as a parting present from his customers and friends. It bore the inscription 'From a few sincere friends and many well-wishers on leaving Dawlish.' Mr. and Mrs.Beachcroft were also presented with a silver butter dish and knife by the hotel staff.

Nevertheless, despite being declared bankrupt in the October of 1901, he is noted in the *East & South Devon Advertiser* in February 1902 as again applying for the license of the Royal Hotel, where the Bench wanted to know more about him. In the box, Beachcroft said he was the son of a Rector and was educated at Newton College under the principal, the Rev. G. Townsend Warner, a Fellow of Jesus College, Cambridge, the Chairman of the Newton Constitutional Club, an ever popular supporter of many sporting games, and president of both the Newton Football Club and the Devon Rugby Union, and on the executive of the English Rugby Union. In addition, The Rev Warner was the Hon. Secretary of the Devon County Cricket Club. With such an endorsement, the license was subsequently transferred to Beachcroft.

Not long after this license transfer both he and his young wife, now just 21, are reported as each putting £1,000 (£60,000 today) into taking on the tenancy and license of the four bedroomed Adelphi Hotel and public house which was situated on the corner of the High Street and Castle Street in Exeter. Unfortunately for them, in February 1903, they now became embroiled in a Licensing Crusade in which a number of licensed establishments were being objected to by the Bishop of Exeter as being in excess of requirements, and that the Bishop believed the Adelphi should only be run as a restaurant.

Beachcroft claimed at this time that his license of the Adelphi was necessary and that he did provide restaurant facilities. His coffee room, he said, was used for up to forty luncheons each day and he additionally served teas, coffee and Bovril in the saloon bar. He also stated his friends played ping-pong in the coffee room after lunch. No decision was apparently made at this time and any decision was noted as deferred.

Subsequently, at the next Justices Court (reported in the *Western Times*, July 6th 1903), his Liquor License was not approved and it was proposed that he permanently hand-over his License to a Mr. Robert Stuckey, a local restaurant owner. At the Exeter Police Court in July 1903 it was stated that the order would be complied with. The following month, again at the Exeter Police Court, it was stated that Mr. Stuckey would be acceptable to take over the License, providing that the conditions laid down for the premises to be used as a restaurant were agreed to.

In November 1903, C B K Beachcroft is again back in Court, this time facing a claim from a mineral water company for an unpaid debt of £34.17s.11d that had been accrued during his time at the Adelphi Hotel. At the hearing Beachcroft states that he is living in lodgings in Exmouth with his wife and family of four young children, Henry George, aged 6, Violet C Beachcroft, 4, Mildred Jeannette Beachcroft, 2, and the newly born Ronald M Beachcroft – who sadly died at 9 weeks (these four children are in addition to the four children with his first wife). He claimed that since the Magistrates 'did him out of the Adelphi' he had done nothing to earn a living, although he had regularly played hockey and cricket throughout the season

Mr. Beachcroft told the Magistrate that he had invested all of his capital in the Adelphi Hotel and 'when the Magistrates had objected to his License for no earthly reason, all of his things had been sold at auction and there was nothing left to pay any of his debts.' The Magistrate commented 'This was a sad case in which a gentleman was able to play like a gentleman, but not pay like a gentleman.'

However, Beachcroft's foray into the licensing trade was still not over. In September 1904 he is appearing at the Dartmouth Magistrate's Licensing Sessions where it is stated that he is the temporary license authority for the King's Arms Hotel and that he was applying for a permanent license. This was a substantial Hotel on the corner of Cowick Street, Exeter, and boasted yards, stables, a Brew House, cellars, a skittle alley and garden. At this time the Brewery Company said they were refusing the license transfer to Mr. Beachcroft from a Miss K Carnell, stating that they believed Beachcroft was not a suitable manager for the hotel and that they had given him notice to quit while offering him a month's salary and a month's board – to be paid in gold.

Appearing for Beachcroft, Mr. Compton absolutely denied that the tenancy had been terminated and Mr. Beachcroft had refused to accept the money. He added that the Brewery Company could not just get rid of him in five minutes. He wanted to argue the transfer and present the full facts. It was then stated that Miss Carnell now wished to return and therefore objected to the permanent transfer of the license to Mr. Beachcroft, The Bench adjourned for three weeks so that proof of termination could be supplied. Transfer of the license was eventually made back to Miss Carnell.

Then, in December 1904 the *Dartmouth & South Hams Chronicle* reported that at the Paignton County Court a case had been listed in which Emily Hooper sued C B Kay for recovery of £3 13s 6d, wages and wages in lieu of notice, board, washing and train fare. The case was marked 'doubtful services.' No appearance was entered, either by the plaintiff or defendant, and the case was struck out.

Enhancing reputation as an entertainer and concert organiser

Throughout his time as a landlord/licensee of the Royal, Adelphi and King's Arms Hotels, C B K Beachcroft was still spending much of his time organising charity and other concerts to raise funds or provide entertainment for local organisations and events, as well as being involved in all his numerous sporting activities. Maybe these were contributing factors to his slide into becoming bankrupt and losing all his capital.

In February 1902 the Annual Dinner of the Exeter Rowing Club took place with a large attendance. It was said that the evening closed with a capital programme of music being rendered by members, including C B K Beachcroft.

At a Trades Exhibition in May 1902 large crowds were drawn to a daily concert by the Viennese Ladies Orchestra, as well as a daily Ping-Pong competition between teams captained by Mr. J Webber and Mr. C B K Beachcroft.

In October the same year the City of Exeter Lodge of the Royal Antidiluvian Order of Buffaloes held a dinner at the Castle Hotel, Exeter, in which Sir Edgar Vincent KCMG, MP, was initiated into the mysteries of the Order. Primo W H Pring (District President) occupied the chair and performed the initiation ceremony in which Sir Vincent received an enthusiastic welcome as a brother. Primo C B K Beachcroft was amongst those present at the dinner and presented to Sir Edgar.

December 1902 has the Exeter Fat Stock Show and Exhibition taking place. Not just about cattle, the event included a Promenade

Concert on Friday December 12th given by the band of the Ist R.V., plus a daily Chantel Concert arranged by C B K Beachcroft, assisted by several well-known professionals.

Other concerts in which CBK was a singer in 1902 were for the Exeter Touring Cycling Club and the Exeter Working-Men's Society, as well as at an open-air concert for the relief of Mrs. Brown whose husband (the one that Beachcroft had tried to save from drowning) had drowned. He also performed a skit entitled *'The Mayor of Mudcomdite'* at a concert on behalf of the Dawlish Swimming Club.

A year later, in February 1903, at the Exeter Rowing Club's Annual Dinner, C B K Beachcroft was amongst those closing the evening by rendering a number of highly comical sketches.

September 1903 sees a Pastoral Concert being held on the Dawlish Lawn to raise funds for the Dawlish Football Club. An excellent programme enjoyed by a large audience was provided by a number of amateur artists. C B K Beachcroft played *'Love's request'* as a cornet solo and later sang *'I want to see the dear old house again.'* Beachcroft's *'Lucky Jim'* was deemed very amusing and received encores.

A subsequent report from the *Western Times* in 1903 mentions an enjoyable programme being rendered by a singing group which included C B K Beachcroft, while the *Exeter and Plymouth Gazette* in Feb 1904 shows Charles Beachcroft performing in The Black Diamond Minstrels quartet at Starcross. Early 1904 also sees him appearing in a smoking concert at the Courtenay Arms Hotel, Starcross, in connection with the H Company 1st R.V. to which

Starcross provided a strong attachment. It was noted in the newspaper report that in order to enable the visitors from Dawlish to remain until the end, the officials of the Great Western Railway arranged for the train leaving Exeter at 11 o'clock to stop at Starcross to take on passengers.

In June 1904 a highly successful open air smoking concert was executed by C B K Beachcroft (who also took part in the concert), this time for B Company 1st R.V. which was also made-up of a strong contingent from Starcross. It was stated that a very pleasant evening was held by all. In the same month a smoking concert was held at the Royal Hotel for the Dawlish Cricket Club. The evening was well attended, with Beachcroft contributing to an excellent musical programme.

Charles Kay, professional entertainer

Certainly his hotel setbacks seem to have spurred him into stepping-up appearances as an amateur variety artist and entertainer at local venues and events in Devon. However, now with little money and creditors on his back, C B K Beachcroft makes the decision to once again try his hand at becoming a full-time professional entertainer on the variety stage – moving to London at the end of 1904.

In 1905, and now back under his original name of Charles Kay (or under the stage name of Jack Trent), he can be found on the professional variety stage, initially in London – noted in late December 1905 in *The Era* as one of the supporting turns at the Chelsea Palace, London, in a review called the '*The Diamond Express* – and then touring in smaller venues around the country such as the Alhambra Theatre of Varieties, Sandgate, Kent where, in March 1906, he appears as a 'Descriptive Vocalist' supporting act. Above him on that bill was a Miss Nettie Franklin & Co. in '*The Bachelor's Dream'*. But more of the Franklin girls later.

Early May 1906 sees *The Era* reporting on the opening night of the new Palace of Varieties, Lydd, Kent, to a crowded house. Performances included Charles Kay, the popular comedian, who performed his topical song, '*The Beautiful Tale of Love*,' gathering fresh laurels at every verse; Sybil Franklin and Company, in 'A Bachelor's Dream; and Harry Wallace, coon singer. Charles Kay eventually went on to have three children with Sybil Franklin, although they were never married).

By August 1906, Kay is again in London, appearing at the

Preserve 22, 1907.

and Agents!

RIKE

the iron is hot, and secure

CHARLES KAY

☙ **THE TYPICAL TOPICAL TALKER** ☙

The Hit of the Bill last week at the Holborn Empire

"A MUDDLED MELODY"

AND

" A BEAUTIFUL TALE OF LOVE."

THIS WEEK

EMPIRE PALACE

Croydon.

" After a WHITE Frost there's always a THAW."

Thanks to Oswald Stoll, Esq., Walter Gibbons, Esq., and Henri Gros, Esq., for Contracts.

AND STILL THEY COME !

What the Press has Said !

Look out for "POSTER-LAND," in preparation.

London and provincial Entr'acte, 21st February, 1907. Image © The British Library Board. All rights reserved. Included with permission of the British Newspaper Archive (www.britishnewspaperarchive.co.uk)

Palace, Tottenham and, by the February of 1907, singing '*Oh, What a Lovely Story*' at the Holborn Empire. Later in the month he takes '*The Typical Topical Talker*' to the Empire Palace, Croydon (see the full page newspaper advert). Comments in 'What the Press has Said' at the foot of the advert noted that 'Three curtain calls at each house tell their own tale.'

In 1907, there are numerous records of Charles Kay performing at theatres around England. In April that year he tops the bill at the Aquarium, Scarborough, and is the chief attraction – and an enormous success – for a seven week run at the South Pavilion, Lowestoft, in July (and said to be causing screams of laughter).

However, it is perhaps the opening of the new Sunderland Empire Palace, also in July 1907, that was perhaps a more memorable one for him. Attended by a large audience – including Sir Ed. Moss and Mr. Oswald Stoll – the theatre's opening included Miss Vesta Tilley (Britain's most popular male impersonator at the time and one of the country's most successful music hall performers),

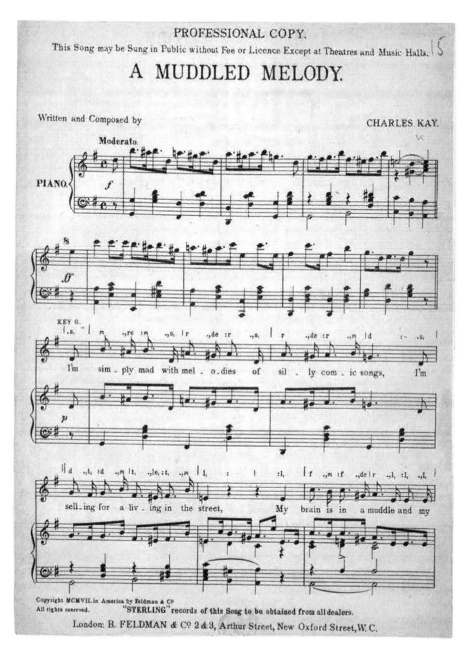

Image © The British Library Board. Song 'A Muddled Melody' written and composed by Charles Kay in 1907. BL Shelfmark H.3984. uu.(15) X 4 pages. Page 1.

Image © The British Library Board. Song 'A Muddled Melody'
written and composed by Charles Kay in 1907. BL Shelfmark H.3984.
uu.(15) X 4 pages. Page 2.

Image © The British Library Board. Song 'A Muddled Melody'
written and composed by Charles Kay in 1907. BL Shelfmark H.3984.
uu.(15) X 4 pages. Page 3.

A MUDDLED MELODY.

1.

I'm simply mad with melodies of silly comic songs—
I'm selling for a living in the street—
My brain is in a muddle and my head is in a whirl,
They're in the mouths of everyone you meet.
Just fancy "Irish Molly" with some "Seaweed" in her hand
"In the valley where the Blue Bird sings,"
Or imagine "Alexander" singing "Birdseed" when he's "Blind,"
With "Rags and Bones" and "Lucky Ducks" and things.

CHORUS.

What's the use of "Putting bits away for rainy days,"
In a little "Bamboo Bungalow" so high?
Why wouldn't "Daddy" leave his "Little wooden hut"?
"There's a girl inside"—that's why.

2.

When "A little boy called Taps" from the famous "Chelsea School"
Says "Stop yer ticklin', Jock," to "Dolly Gray,"
Or he was only "Teasing," "Have a drop o' gin, old dear,"
D'you think that they'd believe him in "Bombay"?
Or if a "Gondolier" said "'Owd yer row" to me,
Or tried to pinch "Ma Daisy" "In the dark,"
I'd seize him by "The Bell and Bush" for "Freedom and Japan,"
And kick him "On the benches in the Park."

CHORUS.

What's the good of "Giving your regards to Leicester Square"
With a "Piccadilly Johnnie" on the spy?
Why can't a married woman leave her "Little wooden hut"?
She gets "Pinched" by the "Slops"—that's why.

3.

Oh, Alice, "Alice, where art thou?" amongst the "Banks and Braes,"
"Ben Bolt" says "Annie Laurie's" missing too;
They're looking for "The Lost Chord" far away from "Home, sweet Home,"
"The Bay of Biscay" ain't no place for you.
I'm "Off to Philadelphia," where "Jack's the boy for work,"
I'm told by "Bonnie Mary of Argyle,"
"Jerusalem," "God save the King," and "Ehren on the Rhine,"
"Killarney," "Killaloe," is more my style.

CHORUS.

What's the good of "Mona" when you've got your "Anchors weighed"?
I'm an "Absent-minded Beggar," "Nelly Bly."
Why did she "Dream that she dwelt in marble halls"?
She's a bloomin' Suffragette—that's why.

4.

Was Huntley Wright or wrong when he said that Edna May?
And if she did, why shouldn't Phyllis Dare?
If the Marie Tempest blew the branches off the Beerbohm Tree,
Was Evie Greene to shoot the Gilbert Hare?
Would you give Mary Moore if she drank the Bernard Beere,
To Seymour (H) extra special in the Strand?
Was Louis Freear freer than she really ought to be?
And why was Wilkie Bard?—you understand.

CHORUS.

Why was Hayden Coffin, and what gave Edmund Payne?
'Cos they'd lent their Vesta Tilley for to dry;
Why do the girls get the Camille Clifford hump?
They ain't copped a lord—that's why.

*Image © The British Library Board. Song 'A Muddled Melody'
written and composed by Charles Kay in 1907. BL Shelfmark H.3984.
uu.(15) X 4 pages. Page 4.*

who headed the bill, receiving thunderous applause. Charles Kay was amongst the evening's performers, rendering an amusing medley of songs past and present, and Miss Lillian Lea, who brought the programme to a close with a pretty scene entitled '*Dear Little Primrose*'

Following his run at The South Pavilion, Lowestoft, as *The Typical Topical Talker*, his song, '*A Muddled Melody*' was purchased by B Feldman, the London music publisher (the published words and music for this song is held in the Music Collection at the British Library, and reproduced with their permission on the previous four pages). The song was reported in *The Era* as 'a great number and was a big success everywhere in London and on the Stoll Tour.'

By November 1907 *The Era* carries the news that Charles Kay, The Typical Topical; Talker, whose song, '*A Muddled Melody*' is such a big success, is starting a long provincial tour at His Majesty's Theatre of Varieties, Walsall, on December 2nd (where he was referred to in the *Walsall Advertiser* as 'six foot of smartness,' and then will be returning to London to open at the London Coliseum, to be followed by a tour of Mr. Stoll's Empires theatres and the syndicate halls, including appearances to audiences at the Bath Halls, Wimbledon and the Crystal Empire, Battersea.

From London, Charles Kay headed to Scotland where he successfully appears at the Glasgow Empire in January 1908, moving down to the Palace Theatre in Leicester, and noted as being assisted by the capital vocalist, Miss Sybil Franklin. During May and June he could be found appearing at the Hackney Empire and then, again, as a very memorable support act, excellent audiences being secured at the Shepherd's Bush Empire, London, in a programme headed by W C Fields – the American comedian, actor, juggler and writer. The Four Emilions appeared as a flying acrobatic act of a high order and Charles Kay, *The Typical Topical Talker*, assisted by Miss Sybil Franklin, found considerable favour.

He is noted later as appearing in Faversham, Kent, as a comedian, then in a November 14th 1908, edition of *The Whistable Times* as at Seasalter Parish Hall and appearing as the 'well-known London comedian' as part of an Amateur Dramatic Society Concert. Later the same year various local newspaper clippings show him as again touring theatres in Kent during August 1908, including the New Pavilion in Tankerton, then moving round the coast to Seasalter, and on to Whitstable and Herne Bay in September.

SEASALTER
AMATEUR DRAMATIC SOCIETY,
A CONCERT
Will be given by the above Society on
Wednesday, Nov. 18ᵗʰ, 1906
In
SERASALTER PARISH HALL
Artists:
Miss NETTIE FRANKLIN, R.A.N.
(Gold Medallist)
Miss A. H. DODMAN, L.R.A.N.
Mr CHARLES KAY
(The well known London Comedian)
Mrs FRANK REEVES
The Whitstable String Band under the
conductorship of Mr. J. J. Hill

Extract from an advert in The Whistatable Times and Herne Bay Herald, November 14th 1908.

During his time at the New Pavillion, Tankerton, the local Whitstable paper from the 8th August comments that 'Large houses were the order of the day. Charles Kay, *The Typical Topical Talker* is, if possible, now more popular than ever. His parody on the '*Old Apple Tree*' is screamingly funny and his references to Tankerton's Dorando (Dorando was an Italian marathon runner who finished first in the 1908 London Olympics, but was later disqualified) and the Slavier Case created quite a furore. An excellent portrait of him appeared in last week's '*The Throne and Country' magazine.*' This weekly title with a 10,000 circulation, was particularly focussed on society, fashion, sport and the theatre. It was regarded as quite an achievement to be featured in it.

Two weeks later, he is again mentioned in the *Whitstable Times* Newspaper as being the Chairman of a Men's Concert organised at the Seasalter Parish Hall by the Rev. T Pitman. The Newspaper described Mr. Charles Kay as 'decidely one of the most popular comedians to have ever visited Whitstable' and who rendered the Star Turn of the evening with four of his funny efforts and teaming with topical and local allusions.'

The Vaudeville page from the 1st August, 1908, issue of 'The Throne and Country', featuring Charles Kay, bottom centre.
Image © The British Library, LOU LON 28 (1908)

As previously mentioned, it is interesting to note that during his theatrical touring as *The Typical Topical Talker* he is frequently shown in the billing as performing on the same bill as, or being assisted by either a Miss Nettie Franklin or a Miss Sybil Franklin.

In early September 1908 Charles Kay is again reported in the local Whitstable newspaper as appearing at the New Pavillion in Jack Rowland's popular Concerts. It was noted that 'Mr. Charles Kay, who again appeared, had his benefit night on Thursday, when there was an excellent house.'

The September 26th 1908 edition of *The Whistable Times* and Herne Bay Herald mentions that he was part of a Grand Farewell Concert at the Assembly Rooms and that audiences never tired of his original humour. The Concert was put together with three of the artists who had achieved much success at the New Pavillion with the assistance of Miss Aubrey Hylton, solo pianist from the Royal Albert and Bechstein Halls. Miss Hedda Hirleman acted as the general director and producer for the evening.

During the Concert Charles Kay sang *'The Beautiful Tale of Love'* and when encored gave the audience *'Girls, Girls, Beautiful Girls'*. Also on the programme was Hedda Hirleman who sang *'Pussy had another sardine'* at the piano and then rendered a duet with Charles Kay entitled *'Nobody knows, nobody cares'*. Both songs were encored. His final song was *'Come and have a drink with me'*.

In the same week as the Concert, Charles Kay can be found playing in various cricket matches in the town. One of the matches was between Herne Bay and the 'Herons'. Described as one of the most interesting matches of the season, in which a feature of the Herons innings was a fine not-out effort by Charles Kay. Indeed, during the cricket week, Kay was praised for a total of five 'not-out' innings.

The following month *The Whitstable Times* and *Herne Bay*

Herald' reports on a cricket match between Whitstable and Herne Bay in which the home team won 'thanks to a fine innings of 36 by Charles Beachy Kay.' Little wonder that he was extremely popular in Whitstable – and it wasn't just for performing on the stage and cricket. January 1909 has him captaining Charles B Kay's XI in a hockey match with the town club. The match resulted in a draw at four goals each. Kay (reported as a former Devon County player) was one of the goal scorers.

While performing for the season in Whitstable, the *Kentish Times and Farmers Gazette* of 3rd October reported that Charles Kay, the popular comedian and a firm favourite in Whitstable, organised another Beauty and Baby Show in the Assembly Halls, Whitstable. Miss Florence West was chosen as the prettiest girl in Whitstable, receiving a gold bangle. A fine one-year old little girl received a gold brooch. The evening concert included Miss Hirlemann, contributing old favourites. Mr. Charles Kay surpassed himself singing *'Sheltering Tree.'*

In February 1909 Charles Kay appears for a week at the Crouch End Hippodrome, London, and is noted as making a big hit with an entirely new song, written and composed by him entitled '*Come and Join the Territorial Army.*' By August 1909 the *Dover Express* has Charles Kay back in Kent and appearing twice nightly at the Palace and Hippodrome, Dover, where he is advertised as the

> Mr. Charles Kay is making a big hit at Crouch End hippodrome, London, this week with an entirely new song, written and composed by him entitled "Come and Join the Territorial Army."

Canterbury Journal, Kentish Times and Farmers' Gazette. 13th February. 1909. Image © The British Library Board.

'Eccentric Comedian'.

Then in October 1909, '*The Western Times*' shows Kay appearing at the Barnfield Hall, Exeter, where they state that the Society Entertainers 'The Pinks' under the direction of Charles Kay, presented their new vaudeville entertainment and noting that Mr. Kay is an old Exonian, and his humorous contributions to the programme were much appreciated. Other members of the programme again included Sybil Franklin.

Later the same month, both Charles Kay and Sybil Franklin are appearing in a *Special Matinee for County Visitors*, again at the Barnfield Hall, where he is billed as Charles B Kay from The Palace, London.

Some eight or nine years after winning the Olympic Gold Medal, and now regularly appearing as Charles Kay, his name starts to frequently appear in articles, clippings and adverts in *The Stage Newspaper, The Era newspaper* and in local UK and London newspapers, particularly from 1910 and continuing until 1919 when he announced in The Stage in 1919 that he was changing his name to Jack Trent - a name which he also used as one of his acting characters during his time touring as Charles Kay. References in The Stage to Jack Trent then continue until the end of 1921.

He is noted as Charles Kay, the Man in Blue, appearing in his Latest Absurdity '*Sexton Blake*', during 1910. For reference, Sexton Blake was a fictional consulting private detective (written about over the years since 1893 by some 200 different authors) with many similarities to Sherlock Holmes. They both operated from London's Baker Street. Both detectives employed a housekeeper, and both had a bloodhound and an assistant.

In the 1911 Census, Charles Kay is listed as lodging at Hercules Villa, Sandown Road, Deal, Kent. His occupation given as Music Hall Artist. His assistant, Sybil Franklin, that he had been touring with for the past few years, is now shown in the Census as Sybil Kay, Music Hall Artist. Also listed in the Census is their three-month old son, John Kay. They had two other children together before John Kay, but these are not mentioned in the Census. Sybil Kay was shown in the Census as being 25 years old at the time – his third 'wife' and 11th child – although they were not married.

Then, in May 1911 the *'Taunton Courier'* writes about an interesting gathering at Bridgewater where employees of the Tone Vale Manufacturing Company assembled for an excellent musical programme and concert, including Charles Kay, to do honour to the principals of the company – Messrs H J Van Troup and W H J Masding – who were a large employer of labour in Taunton, and active in public life in the town.

Back in Devon in November 1911, the *North Devon Journal* has a report in the paper stating that 'Mr. Charles Kay, the well-known Devon comedian, who on a visit to Barnstable Picturedrome last Easter was such a success, that he is again visiting the Picturedrome this week and, with his original comic songs, is once more proving a great attraction.'

A prominent variety artist and well-loved comedian

By now, Charles Kay has become regarded as a prominent music hall variety artist and touring theatre company manager and appears regularly in both the pages of *The Stage* and *The Era*. He toured a great many of the major provincial and London theatres with sketches/shows that he had either written and/or produced himself, including recognised successes such as: '*Do be Careful*', '*Detective Copp*', '*Kiss in the Ring*' and '*Little Babette*'.

The Stage newspaper variously describes him over the years as the possessor of a fine appearance, charming, charismatic, a real and original comedian of great experience, intensely funny, a popular favourite with young and old, while his character impersonations, particularly clerical impersonations, were described as most droll.

The *Teignmouth Gazette* of March 12th 1913, reports Charles Kay as an enormous success in '*The Simple Little Curate*', going on to describe him as 'a magnificent turn, his brilliant patter and singing being

Charles Kay, taken from a promotional stage postcard kept by his daughter, Dorothy, and believed to have been photographed in 1914

the cause of great applause'.

In April 1913 he is mentioned in the *Sussex Agricultural Express* as appearing, for the first time, with Lola Trent in a humorous interlude '*Billy the Brokers Man*' – described as an amusing discourse on money and a parody of Alexander's Rag Time Band.

July 1913 has *The Era* reporting that the clever comedian, Charles kay, was appearing at the Pavilion, Rouken Glen, Glasgow, for the season, managing the Rouken Glen Entertainers and had made a very great personal success with '*Who killed Ragtime*', which was declared the hit of the whole programme. In September he is appearing with Tom Johnson's 'Yachtsmen,' drawing big audiences at The Castle, Aberystwyth. 'Charles Kay, who's songs are clever and original made a big hit with '*John Bull*' and '*A Dream of the Castle*'. His work was said to be always refreshing and up-to-date.

Then, in December 1913, Charles Kay and Carson Hicks appear in '*Tommy Tucker*' at the Royal Princess's Theatre, Glasgow, as a couple of racing tipsters and have a large share in the unravelling of the Baron's wicked plot to keep Tommy out of his estate. *The Era* reported that they were clever comedians who introduce a lot of funny business and are never at a loss.

There can be little doubt that Charles Kay was a great success over the years in pantomime, playing parts such as the Baron Bunkum, the wicked uncle in '*Babes in the Wood*', the Baron in '*Cinderella*', and Will Atkins in '*Robinson Crusoe*'. In 1912 he was appearing as the Mayor of Muddleup in '*The House that Jack Built*' pantomime at the Theatre Royal Bradford, which ran for nine weeks. The *Yorkshire Evening Post* stated that Charles Kay as the Mayor was a capital actor of eccentric parts. In addition, The *Halifax Guardian* at that time describes his portrayal of the Mayor as 'leaving nothing to be desired, having a splendid physique, set-off to advantage by his splendid mayoral robes.' He also had 15 successful weeks of pantomime at the Princess's Theatre, Glasgow in 1913 and into 1914.

In April 1914 the *Nottingham Evening Post* carries an advert for a Special Easter Holiday Attraction at Colwick Park, Nottingham, in which Charles Kay, the popular favourite comedian, direct from his latest success at the Princesses Theatre, Glasgow, has been specially engaged. September of the same year sees another advert in the same newspaper saying 'You must come to Olympia Trent Bridge this week to see the 'Dandy Boys' with Charles Kay.

In *The Stage* Newspaper of May 1914 there is a report of Charles Kay appearing at The Oxford, London, in '*The Big Policeman and his Little Black Cat*', and being singled out for commendation and special mention as the Policeman.

A couple of months later, in July the same year, he is again appearing as the 'excellently humorous Policeman', in the same show, this time at the Chiswick Empire, London. He was to follow this by appearing in '*Miss Paris in London*', also at the Chiswick Empire.

Indeed in the previous month, this same show, promoted as a Champagne Review, had appeared at The Palace, Hull, where the *Hull Daily Mail* reported that this was the most gigantic production of its kind seen in Hull for a long time. On the stage were 60 artists jostling each other in a mad rush to provide something in the gaiety line and commenting that the show has no plot and no sense – but there is plenty of fun. 'Venus-like figures display to advantage Parisian gowns, whilst others disport themselves in much flimsy attire; and in two scenes a few pairs of sturdy legs were kicked about.'

The report goes on to say that 'there is plenty of wayward naughtiness to set even the most conservative Puritan mind pondering. The jokes – there are hundreds of them – are not all consistent with good taste.' The show also included a magnificent water spectacle. Charles Kay is particularly noted as the pick of the bunch amongst the male comedians.

During the time that '*Miss Paris in London*' Revue was at the Chiswick Empire, a cricket team from the show put together by Charles Kay opposed the Hall City police at cricket and won easily. The '*Miss Paris*' team scored 146 runs for one wicket. Charles Kay was not out. A subsequent match was played against the Ilford Police, resulting in a draw. Charles Kay scored 19.

Apart from his acting and comedy roles, Charles Kay also seems to have been quite a singer, songwriter and musical performer. His rendering of '*I know where the Flies go*' was said to be sung by everybody. His singing of '*Same to you with knobs on*' was a sure hit, and he performed his song '*The New Humpty Dumpty*' in Bath in January 1915 with much acclaim.

The *New Devon Journal*, in a later report stated that from 1905 he appeared at the Palace Coliseum and London Syndicate halls, and all the principal theatres in Great Britain under the Moss and

Stoll management, and also in South Africa. He was said to write all his own songs.

It is perhaps worth noting that Moss Empires was a British company formed in Edinburgh from the merger of the theatre companies owned by Sir Edward Moss, Richard Thornton and Sir Oswald Stoll in 1899, so creating the largest British chain of variety theatres and music halls. The business was very successful, with major variety theatres in almost every city in Great Britain and Ireland, and was advertised as the largest theatre group in the world.

A heartless desertion

During the period of his successes and mentions in *The Stage* Charles Kay had three major partners, whose stage names were firstly, Sybil Franklin, followed by Lola Trent, and then later, Sadie Logan.

Charles Kay apparently first met Eliza Sybil Franklin when she was just 16 – while he was still married and having children with his wife Carrie. Her uncle was John Franklin, the famous tragedian, who didn't want his niece to be an actress at all, although he did give her small parts in his own touring company. By 1904 at the age of 19, she and her sister Nettie, had their own company touring small theatres. Sybil travelled the same theatres and venues around the country with him from 1905/6 when she was 21. This was about the same time he had become a professional entertainer. As previously mentioned, she was shown on theatre bills with him over the next few years, appearing as Sybil Franklin with her own comedy or musical turns, or as being his assistant.

In October 1909 she appears at Plymouth with Charles Kay, where she is noted 'as a light comedienne' and that he was 'responsible for some humorous contributions from his own pen.' Later the same month she is reported as being 'a charming comedienne, who has only just returned from South Africa.' It is not known whether Charles had also been to South Africa with her (although there is a shipping record of a Charles Kay travelling to South Africa in early October 1909). Later reports also indicated that he had at one time performed in South Africa. They certainly became very close as she went on to have three children with him

Extract from The Daily Herald, Adelaide, 17th January 1912. Image reproduced with permission of the National Library of Australia

by the time she was 25.

Then in December 1911, while appearing at the King's Theatre, Ramsgate, Charles Beachy Kay is approached by a Detective Sergeant Duff and served with a summons to 'show cause why he should not contribute to the support of his three children by Sybil Franklin'. The latest of these being just a few months old.

In the subsequent court hearing at Ramsgate Police Court, Mr. Robinson, who appeared for Eliza Sybil Franklin, stated that the defendant described himself as an original and versatile comedian, although he believed he was originally a solicitor and had previously come into a lot of money, had gone through all of it, and was now on the stage as a comedian. The local Ramsgate newspaper (also re-reported as far afield as the *The Daily Herald*, Adelaide), headlined the court report as a 'Heartless Desertion' and an extraordinary story (See illustration above).

In that report, Robinson goes on describe some of the defendant's amours with other women before he met the complainant when she was just 16, and ran away with her when she was 21, subsequently living together as man and wife for six years and had three children He described how Charles Kay had deserted Miss Franklin for a young girl of 19 (Florrie Lane, as described in the next chapter) and had told her as a source of consolation that it was 'the cry of nature', and stating in one of his letters to her that 'Of course, it is very hard on you and you are naturally very sorry. It is nature's cry and cannot be helped. I cannot imagine you marrying yourself to just one man who is now madly in love with another woman.'

In another letter to Miss Franklin, Kay had said she could have no idea of the 'beautiful disposition and fascinating ways of his other charmer', adding that it was no doubt a good quality to be a perfect mother, but when the father was not perfect and, was as she knew, peculiar, and was made to suffer from the mother's perfectness, it was a hopeless case. Mr. Robinson said Kay made use of the statement that 'Any girl could get a man, but was she clever enough to keep him'? It was said that this was the sort of heartless letters that the defendant wrote to the woman who was the mother of his three children.

Robinson than went on to prove the defendants earnings, stating that Kay was currently earning about £6 a week in pantomime (over £400 in 2016) and that over the year his average earnings were nearer £4 per week. The Bench proceeded to make an order for the defendant to pay five shillings a week for each of his three children until they were 16 years of age, as well as all court costs and solicitors fees.

At the time of the court hearing in December 1911, Charles Kay was already touring on stage with his new stage partner, Lola Trent.

Charles Kay and Lola Trent

Picture shows an early stage photo of Florrie Kay/Lola Trent, nee Florrie Lane, when she was 21.

Lola Trent's maiden name was Florrie Lane. She had run away from home in 1911 to join his touring cast while he was playing in Nottingham. Florrie was only a young 17 year old girl at the time and soon adopted the stage name Lola Trent. In February 1913 they had a daughter together, christened as Dorothy Florence Kay, and two years later a son, Reginald. Parents on the birth certificates in each case were given as Charles Beachcroft Kay and Florrie Kay (nee Lane), although it is difficult to find any official record of them actually being married.

Just two months after having their daughter, Charles Kay and Lola Trent (her stage name) are showing in the *Sussex Agricultural Express* as the 'Starring Engagement' at the County Theatre, Lewes. Charles Kay is described as the 'Original Comedy Merchant' in all his latest successes – including an amusing discourse on money, while Lola Trent and partner perform in their humorous interlude '*Billy, the Broker's Man*'.

Baby Dorothy toured with them for the first few months, being

Advertisement from the Sussex
Agricultural Express - Friday 11 April
1913. Image © Johnston Press plc. Image
created courtesy of the British Library Board.

placed in a props basket to sleep while they were on stage, before then going to live and stay with her grandmother in Nottingham until she was eight. Reginald was placed with a foster family.

Not long after their success in Lewes, Charles Kay and Lola Trent are performing together in '*A Dark Secret*' at the Leicester Pavilion while, in November 1913, they are announcing their new county theatres tour, as well as a Christmas Panto contract for that year at the Princesses Theatre, Glasgow. The Panto successfully ran for 15 weeks in Glasgow, with Charles Kay billed as the Original Comedian and Lola Trent presenting her Comedy Interludes.

By November 1914 Charles Kay can be found being complemented on the success of his new artistically and carefully staged musical, '*The Allies Musical*'. It was noted that 'Mr. Kay introduced a well-arranged vocal quartet, with a vein of comedy throughout the entertainment.'

In December 1914 they were performing together in Bath, with Kay successfully playing the Baron in Cinderella at the Theatre

Royal. A few weeks later it is noted that Charles Kay won a prize for the highest billiards break in a match between the company of Cinderella and the gentlemen of Bath, held at the Assembly Rooms. This was followed by a supper and dance for over 100 people during which Charles Kay sang his new song, '*The New Humpty Dumpty*'.

March 1915 sees Charles Kay announcing that he would be touring with his new and original review, '*Do be Careful*', in which he claimed he would have a cast of over 30 London artists.

The following month sees the first newspaper report of this review, stating that Charles Kay's enormously successful production of '*Do be Careful*', written,

Lola Trent (nee Florrie Lane) appeared regularly with Charles Kay in pantomime, as in this signed picture to him when she was playing the part of Will Scarlett.

composed and invented by himself, was presented for the first time at the Coliseum, Bury St. Edmunds. The cast included Lola Trent. There were said to be packed houses, full of screams, yells and rounds of applause.

In May 1915, after a preliminary run in the provinces Charles Kay produced '*Do be Careful*' in London for the first time. Kay

111

Advertisement from 'The Bure Free Press'. Saturday April 3rd, 1915.
Image © The British Library Board. All rights reserved. Included with permission of the British Newspaper Archive (www. britishnewspaperarchive.co.uk)

played Gentleman Jack; Jack's sister Flash Kate, is played by Lola Trent. 'Charles Kay does his share as Gentleman Jack with a fair measure of success. Miss Lola Trent makes the most of Kate Flash.'

Later that same year, in October 1915, it was announced that the Trents of *'Detective Copp'* fame had postponed all engagements due to the serious illness of Lola Trent (this would have been when she was pregnant with their son Reginald). They were in rehearsals at the Hippodrome, Wrexham, at the time. The previous week they were performing in Aldershot.

That same month *The Stage* Newspaper, in a report called 'Actors in the War' announces that Charles Kay had applied for a commission in the Army Service Corps, and had been offered a commission in the Devon Regiment. There appears to be no references at this time as to whether this was taken up, although later reports in August 1918 stated that he had been claimed by the military.

In the early part of 1916 *The Stage* carries an advert announcing Charles Kay's *New Original Revue*, a novelty revue in three scenes with a dramatic plot, and a cast of 25 London artists.

In May 1916, they are again performing together (as The Trents) in *'Detective Copp'* this time at the Exeter Hippodrome, where the local newspaper writes; 'There is considerable local interest centred around the visit of The Trents from the Oxford, London, by means of the part of Charles being taken by Mr. Charlie Beachcroft, who was at one time well-known in athletic circles. In their turns, for there are two, Charles and his lady colleague Lola should be extremely acceptable, for the absurdity of their farcical little sketch, '*Detective Copp*' which can be recommended as a splendid antidote to a 'fit of the blues'. It arouses hearty laughter.

Equally acceptable was their new version of '*In the shade of the old apple tree*' in which 'they

A promotional postcard showing Charles Kay and Lola Trent appearing as The Trents in 'Detective Copp.,

introduce several topical skits, had a hit at the Government, as well as a word of praise for Devon hero Buller, and our brave Tommies.'

They were still performing together in March 1917 as the Trents when they were noted as again playing their skit '*Detective Copp*' at the Casino, Aberdeen, with plenty of success, and again in October 1917 where the Trents are appearing in Carlisle as part of the Macnaughton Tour

Charles Kay and Lola Trent certainly toured Moss and Stoll theatres (the largest British chain of variety theatres and music halls at that time) throughout the UK extensively from 1913 through to the end of 1917 – sometimes under the name of The Trents or as Jack and Lola Trent – but then there are no further references to Charles Kay, Lola Trent or The Trents during 1918, except for a paragraph in the *Hull Daily Mail* in August that year welcoming the return of '*The Summits*', Albert Lyon's Premier Concert Party, 'lest the service of Jack Trent who has been claimed by the military authorities.'

At some stage during 1918, Charles Kay and Lola Trent (Florrie Lane) spilt up. Florrie and her daughter Dorothy returned to live with her mother in Nottingham, with the young Dorothy later recalling that at the time she can remember hiding in the kitchen with her mother while Charles was banging on the front door demanding to see them. They had to pretend that nobody was at home.

Eighteen months later in Dover, Florrie Lane was to marry an Albert Christian Oesch, son of a Swiss head waiter at a leading Brighton hotel, with whom she went on to have another daughter, Pamela. The hotel was one that Charles Kay and Lola Trent had frequently stayed in when they were performing in Brighton.

Charles Kay under another name

No other newspaper references to Charles Kay or Jack Trent can be found in 1918. Maybe he was 'claimed by the military' as stated in the Hull newspaper, although no army records have been found for him during the year in question. It was not until early 1919, that Charles Kay now re-appears, announcing in *The Stage* that he was officially changing his name to Jack Trent. In April of that year, as Jack Trent, he then places an advert in *The Stage* inviting managers who want versatility to fill their programmes to look at his experience and what he can offer.

The advert also includes the contact details as Jack Trent and Sadie. Throughout 1919 he tours successfully under the name of Jack Trent, sometimes with a mention in the programme amongst other cast members, the name of Sadie Logan.

March 1919 sees the prominent character of Colonel Wood at the Royal County, Bedford, in '*Kiss in the Ring*' being ably played by Jack Trent, who is the 'possessor of a fine appearance and a clear oratory. As a character study his Colonel is a real gem, whilst his love scenes cause hearty laughter.'

The following month, Jack Trent is known to have played the title role in his own act '*Detective Copp*' at the Grand Theatre, Halifax, while in September 1919, Jack Trent, who is said to be a favourite on the island (Isle of Wight) brings a first class company and his original character impersonations, including '*Colonel Percy*' and '*The Curate*' both of which were said to be delighting full houses.

Then in December 1919 Jack Trent, who had by then toured

JACK TRENT

(The Acme of Versatility)

Following my success as **"Colonel Wood"** in **"Kiss in the Ring"** 1919, **"P. G. Simpson"** in **"Little Babette,"** 1919 (N.B. - Wilfred Dane, Esq., the Author and Composer) writes: "Dear Jack, you are the best 'Simpson' I have ever had"); and **"Timothy Ruskin"** in Arthur G Hart's **"You're Spotted"** 1919.

Now specially engaged by ***Britain's Greatest Film Comedian***

PIMPLE

To play the part of **"Captain Raffles"** In the revised edition of his "Top of the Bill" production

"FATHER"

An instantaneous success, personally congratulated by Mr. and Mrs. Fred Evans and other artists on the bill at the EMPIRE, GLASGOW, also

MISS

SADIE LOGAN

(Late "Belle" in "You're Spotted")

Now playing **"Miss West"** in **"Father"**.

Advertisement extract from The Stage in December 1919

during the year with his '*Kiss in the Ring*' revue as Colonel Christopher Wood, is noted to have taken up the part of Timothy Ruskin in 'You're Spotted' at short notice , and gave an excellent performance. It was also noted that Mr. Trent was to play Will Atkins in Mr. Arthur G Hart's 'Robinson Crusoe' pantomime at Christmas.

Following Jack Trent's success as Colonel Wood in '*Kiss in the Ring*' and as P G Simpson in '*Little Babette*' the author and composer Wilfred Dane wrote that Jack was the best Simpson he had ever had, while an advert in The Stage announces that Jack Trent had been specially engaged to play the part of Captain Raffles in '*Father*', with Sadie Logan as '*Miss West*'.

It was also noted in December 1919 that the Vaudeville Company of Artists, including Jack Trent and Sadie, had been specially selected by the military authorities to entertain the troops during Christmas and the New Year.

The *Hartlepool Mail* in February 1920 shows that '*Robinson*

Crusoe' is now appearing at the Grand Theatre, Hartlepool, where Jack Trent, playing a pirate, contributed largely to the fun. *'Robinson Crusoe'*, again including Jack Trent, also travels to the Pavillion Theatre, Ashington, Northumberland, in the early part of 1920.

In May 1920 it is announced in *The Stage* that Jack Trent and Sadie Logan had become engaged. She is later described as a dainty and versatile soubrette specialising in ragtime and in low comedy. It was stated at the time that Jack Trent was a comedian of great experience and was a popular favourite with both young and old. As a parson, he was said to be intensely funny and to get a tumultuous recall. His charming manner made him a great favourite. He was a real comedian. It was also noted that Sadie Logan caused screams as a comedy slave.

There is a further reference in the early part of 1920 to Jack Trent and Sadie as being part of an excellent programme at the Bijou Theatre, Hull, in which they are shown as performing a novel act. This was all part of a touring burlesque show. In July 1920 he is shown as being the manager and comedian producer for Messrs Dobson's company and as having success with a new song. By August 1920, Jack Trent and Sadie Logan are performing at the Savoy Theatres.

They are also noted during 1920 as appearing at the Brighton Beach Pavillion. Jack Trent is described as a host in himself in his comic numbers and his character studies, particularly his clerical impersonations are most droll. *'I know where the Flies go'* will be sung by everybody.

In December that year in Dawlish, Baron Bunkum, the wicked uncle in '*Babes in the Wood*', is an enormous success and capitally impersonated by Jack Trent, whose song '*We'll be welcoming the Flies back*' and whose stump oratory are ably rendered. Other parts include Sadie Logan. The company then proceeded to Exeter (with Jack Trent now playing the part of the Baron) and Taunton as part of a nine week panto tour which included successes in Jersey, Guernsey, Bognor, Chichester and Chepstow – and it was still running in March 1921, appearing at the Palace Theatre, Wells, with Jack Trent this time playing one of the Robbers.

By June 1921, Jack Trent and Sadie Logan are noted as a great success with their own numbers in their summer tour with Jack Sheppard's Summer season. Sadie Logan is said to render two low comedy studies with a rare touch of originality and Jack Trent, comedian, is claimed to be representative of the best in his line – a clever and versatile artist. There are also references to the song '*Same to you with knobs on*' which was proving a hit with numerous artists. Among its singers are Jack Trent and Sadie.

In July 1921 Jack Trent, character comedian and songwriter from The Palace, The Oxford, The Savoy and South African tours, is

One of several adverts placed in The Stage during the autumn of 1921

118

shown as on tour with 'Sadie Logan, versatile soubrette, ragtime and low comedy – two artists with a reputation. Currently at Batley, next week Taunton.'

Throughout much of 1921 they are at various times mentioned in *The Stage* or in newspaper cuttings as either touring with their Great Burlesque '*The Colonel and the Yorkshire Lass*' – variously described as a sure laughing success – or advertising in *The Stage* (see example) for theatre vacancies.

Their final performance together in England in '*The Colonel and the Yorkshire Lass*' is in November 1921 at the Palace Theatre, Wells, Somerset, where they are billed as from The Palace, The Oxford and the Savoy Theatres in London. Their performances were described as an enormous success.

One further reference to Jack Trent in 1921 can be found in an advertisement in the *Wells Journal* of 11th November, announcing that Mr. Jack Trent (Carlton Fredericks favourite comedian) late from '*Little Babette*' and '*Babes in the Wood*' companies who will be presenting the Great Ted Gillard (Light-weight boxing champion of Somerset) who will challenge all comers and give a Grand Exhibition of Boxing. This is again at the Palace Theatre in Wells.

A new life in Australia

There are no further references to Jack Trent and/or Sadie Logan performing on stage in the UK after November 1921. Passenger lists however show Charles Beachy Kay and a Violet Gertrude Kay, aged 21, (shown as his 'wife') emigrating to Sydney, Australia, on the P&O line ship the S S Borda on the 22nd December 1921. His occupation is shown as variety artist. It is noted that he gives his age in the passenger manifest as 42. His actual age at this time was 51. It is not possible to know whether his young 'wife' new his true age.

Pictured is the S S Borda which was used as an immigration liner to Australia between 1920 and 1923. Charles and Violet Kay were travelling as unassisted passengers. That is, they paid their own fare.

Once in Australia, Jack Trent (the stage name in Australia of Charles Kay) and Sadie Logan (the stage name of Violet Kay) are signed to Sir Benjamin Fuller's theatre circuit and over the coming years successfully tour Fuller's dozen or so permanent vaudeville theatres throughout Australia and New Zealand.

A musician himself and interested in theatres, Sir Benjamin controlled an organisation which for many years dominated the world of entertainment in both Australia and New Zealand. His success is said to have been down to his knack of knowing what the public wanted to see on stage.

Sadie Logan, Charles Kay's partner/wife is often referred to in Australian newspaper reports as a character comedienne from the Coliseum and Palladium Theatres, London.

Although it was mid-January 1922 before the couple arrived in Australia, they were already appearing on stage at the Fuller's Theatre in Sydney, in the February where the *Hebrew Standard* of Australia stated that 'An attractive programme arranged at the theatre is proving the most fascinating and popular entertainment in Sydney under the able management of B and J Fuller. Jack Trent and Sadie are included in the list of stars.'

In early March of the same year *The Williamstown Chronicle* reported that, 'Jack Trent, of Trent and Sadie, the English comedy artists, are now appearing at the Bijou Theatre, Williamstown, where his company of selected variety artists are breaking all records for the Australian YMCA at Bulford, Salisbury Plain, Worminster, Sutton Veney, Heylesbury, Hartcotte, etc.

Later in March they were found performing at the King's

Theatre, Adelaide,' while the *Argus* mentions a special April Easter programme being presented at the Bijou Theatre, Melbourne, with the report saying 'On Saturday at the matinee and evening performances, Jack Trent and Sadie, English sketch artists, provided a very bright turn.' They returned to Adelaide in December 1922, this time appearing at the Majestic Theatre, and were also specially engaged to entertain the Aussies for the New Year.

In January 1923 they are both featuring in the Shaftesbury Variety Show in Perth, moving on by March to the Luxor Theatre, Perth, where they were billed as 'the favourite comedians, Jack Trent with Sadie'.

Under the heading 'Bargain Matinee' in the May 4th, 1923 issue of *Westralian Worker*, they are then shown as appearing in Fuller's New Revue Company at the King's Theatre, Adelaide, and billed as the first appearance at the theatre of Jack Trent and Sadie – direct from London - England's Premier Vocal and Comedy Act. This is followed by 'Jack Trent and Sadie, the clever English comedy entertainers, who will this week be seen in another screamingly funny sketch, '*The Major and the WAAC*', at the Shaftesbury Theatre, Perth.

In June 1923 they are once again back in Perth and reported in the *Daily News* as follows: 'The last two nights of an excellent variety bill were presented at the Shaftesbury Theatre, Perth. The cyclonic comedy duo, Jack Trent and Sadie, presented (by special request) their comedy sketch '*The Colonel and the Yorkshire Lass*'.

Other success soon followed, as seen in these two reports from the *Cairns Post* show. 'There was another triumph for Jack Trent and Sadie at the Palace Theatre, Cairns, last night. Patrons cannot get enough of the fine material these two popular artists are providing. Encore after encore greeted their turn last night. Tomorrow is their last night in Cairns, those who have not seen this talented duo, should not miss the last two nights.

The same newspaper later noted 'Messrs. Nicholls and Trent presented a fine musical comedy entitled '*Peaches and Pears*' at the Criterion Hall, Narandera. The show embraces operatic numbers, mirth, melody, dancing and novelty. Well-known Vaudeville artists included Jack Trent, a most versatile artist and Charlie Kay, the fun merchant.'

Charles Kay seems to have been well-in with Sir Benjamin and in 1924 is to be found playing cricket for Sir Benjamin Fuller's XI cricket team in a number of charity matches in New Zealand – even though he would by now have been fifty-four years old. A report in the *Exeter and Plymouth Gazette* in February 1924 records him as playing cricket for Sir Benjamin Fuller's XI against the Veterans at Christchurch, New Zealand, scoring 57 out of the team's 240 runs. His hits included ten fours and several sixes. At Dunedin the previous week he took six wickets for 23 and scored 11. Against Christchurch he took three wickets for 14.

In February 1925, the *Mayborough Chronicle* announces that a Special Starring Engagement of Jack Trent and Sadie, one of the most consistent Vaudeville Acts imported by Sir Ben Fuller for their circuit of Theatres all over Australia, had been arranged.

A very insightful review of the couple was to appear in June 1925. 'A rare and laughable mixture of dignity and impudence' is what Sir Benjamin Fuller said of the performance of Jack Trent and Sadie, who opened the season at the Palace with their great burlesque *'The Colonel and the Yorkshire lass'* Speaking of Mr. Trent the *Sydney Sun* said Jack Tent, of the well-known comedy act 'Jack Trent and Sadie' is an interesting personality as before entering the theatrical profession he made a name for himself in the sporting world.

Back at the Luxor Theatre, Perth (a 3,000 seat theatre), in January 1926, the *Daily News*, Perth, reported that 'The comedy provided by Jack Trent and Sadie was among the bill's most entertaining features. In the sketch 'The Parson and the Maid' the popular couple were in fun making mood and their humorous sullies and entertaining quips were always laughable.'

In February 1926, the same newspaper reports on the 12 February that there were 'Shrieks of laughter from Jack Trent and Sadie, the popular comedy couple appearing at the Luxor.' The following day, the newspaper said that 'Jack Trent and Sadie contributed a dual act entitled 'Sadie meets the Train' in which humor was the predominating feature. They also sang new verses to the popular song *'Show me the way to go home'*. They were given an ovation.

However, as already mentioned earlier, it was not only in the theatre that the couple were making their name. While appearing at the Luxor in Perth, the *Daily News* stated that 'A most enjoyable picnic and cricket outing organized by Messrs. J Homy, Jack Trent (Luxor Theatre) and Mr. W Lowe (of the HM Hotel) took place at Bicton, the journey being made by launch. Over 60 ladies and gentlemen enjoyed the excellent outing. The Luxor team easily defeated their opponents at cricket.' A few days before this report, the newspaper had noted that 'Mr. Jack Trent's XI cricket team and picnic party had left the jetty by special launch for a cricket match against Coo-ce City and His Majesty's.

In December 1926 Jack Trent is appearing in the Christmas pantomime, Robinson Crusoe, at the open-air Cremorne Theatre, Brisbane. The pantomime commenced its run with a matinee at which Father Christmas presented a free gift to all children under 12 years of age.

A change of partners and a move into radio

In February 1927, but now with no mentions of Sadie since late 1926 (newspaper searches indicate that she may have left the stage and possibly married), The *Cairns Post* announces that 'Jack Trent, now appearing with Stan Iveson, opened at the Palace Theatre on Tuesday and received a splendid reception for their sensational vaudeville act, attracting a big audience. They presented for the first time out of the Capital City, their screamingly funny burlesque, '*The Army and the Navy*', which is indeed one of the finest comedy sketches seen in Cairns.

A few days later, the same newspaper says 'Jack Trent and Stan Iveson, direct from an 8 weeks session at the Tivoli and Cremorne Theatres, Brisbane, are appearing at the Palace Theatre, stating that their performance is 'The greatest Comedy Contrast in Vaudeville'. They are presenting the screamingly funny Burlesque '*The Army and the Navy.*'

The following week, the two popular vaudeville artists, Jack Trent and Stan Iveson, appeared in an entire change of programme, the leading item of which is the screamingly funny burlesque entitled '*A Naval and Military Muddle.*'

This programme was then changed for the week after to '*A Clerical Error*' featuring Jack Trent as the vicar of 'Slopton-on-Slush' and Stan Iveson as 'The Butler'. Audiences were told to look out for their screamingly funny version of '*The Prisoner's Song*'.

By April 1927, *The Queensland Times* is reporting that Jack Trent, the English comedian is now appearing at the Martoo's Olympia Theatre, with his popular burlesque, '*The Vicar of Fun.*'

Then in May, The *Brisbane Courier* reports on a monster vaudeville entertainment under the auspices of the R.A.O.B. which was held at the Oddfellows' Hall. 'Jack Trent as the vicar was one of the prominent successes of the evening. Jack Trent, also acting as the stage manager, kept the entertainment moving briskly.'

September 1927 sees another change of partner, this time for a young lady. *The Maitland Daily Mercury* announced that Miss May Kenneth, a comedienne direct from South African Theatre, made her first appearance. '*Catch Me*' was well given, and she further pleased in association with Jack Trent. They gave some clever patter. Mr. Trent proved his ability as a character comedian.

By October and November 1927, Jack Trent, together with Miss May Kenneth, are now regularly appearing together on Night Radio 353 and Sydney 2BL (originally set-up as 2SB in 1923 and becoming 2BL in 1924, only the second official radio station to be licensed in Australia), with a regular light entertainment programme – presenting burlesque and songs on the radio at 10.05 pm one week, a Humorous Interlude the next, a musical comedy act, and so on.

There were other interesting newspaper reports in November 1927, namely from the *Register* which commented: 'Mr. Jack Trent, who made his first radio appearance at 2BL during the past week, has a big reputation in England as a cricketer. Playing regular cricket for 19 years, he scored 17,352 runs, played 126 not out innings, and notched 12 centuries and 82 scores over 50 to 100. He tells an amusing story of his first broadcasting experience in Australia. A show was being broadcast from a theatre, and at the conclusion of his turn the curtain came down rather quickly, hitting

Mr. Trent on the face. Mr. Trent, forgetful of the fact that the microphone was in front of him, then proceeded to abuse stage staff in lurid terms, every word of which went out over the air. This story was told before Mr. Trent had done his first transmission for 2BL. Consequently the cautious announcer on duty instructed the operator to be ready to switch off in case of accidents.

In another biographical report in November 1927 the *Referee* paper stated that 'It may not be generally known but Jack Trent, the well-known vaudeville artist, is Mr. C Beachcroft Kay, the old Devonshire cricketer, who was a prolific scorer in England. He has appeared at every theatre of note in Australia, New Zealand, and South Africa since arriving in Australia in 1922 for Sir Benjamin Fuller.

A final reference to Charles Kay in Australia is to be found in the *Western Morning News and Mercury* on October 9th 1928, announcing that Charles Kay, actor and comedian, had died in Melbourne, Australia, after suffering from pneumonia. He was described as a well-known athlete and a good cricket and hockey player. He was 58 years old at the time of his death.

Charles 'Beachy' Kay certainly seems to have been something of a ladies man and looks to have fathered thirteen or more children with at least six different (young) 'wives' over a period of 25 or so years. With many athletic successes across a variety of sports – including his Olympic Gold Medal – and then over 20 years on the professional stage, he can perhaps best be summed-up in cricketing terms as 'having had a very good innings.'

Appendix I

Theatres, venues and towns in the UK played by Charles Kay

Alhambra Theatre of Varieties, Sandgate

Barnfield Hall, Exeter

Barnstable Picturedrome

Baths Hall, Wimbledon

Bijou Theatre, Hull

Brighton Beach Pavilion

Casino, Aberdeen

Chelse Palace, London

Chiswick Empire, London

Coliseum, Bury St Edmunds

Colwick Park, Nottingham

Crouch End Hippodrome, London

County Theatre, Lewes

Empire Palace, Croydon

Empire Theatre, Coventry

Empire Theatre, Nottingham

Grand Theatre, Halifax

Grand Theatre, Hartlepool

Hackney Empire, London

Hippodrome, Exeter

Hippodrome, Wrexham

Holborn Empire, London

King's Theatre, Ramsgate

Leicester Pavilion

London Syndicate Halls

Olympia Trent Bridge, Nottingham

New Pavilion, Tankerton

Palace and Hippodrome, Dover

Palace Coliseum, London

Palace Theatre, London

Palace Theatre, Wells

Pavilion Theatre, Ashington

Princesses Theatre, Glasgow

Savoy Theatre

Seasalter Parish Hall

Shepherds Bush Empire, London

Theatre Royal, Bath

Theatre Royal, Bradford

The Oxford, London

The Palace, Hull

The Palace, London

The Palace, Tottenham

Other towns known to have been played by Charles kay include:

Aldershot

Batley

Bognor

Bridgewater

Chepstow

Chichester

Dawlish

Deal

Faversham

Guernsey

Herne Bay

Isle of Wight

Jersey

Starcross

Taunton

Whitstable

Appendix II

Skits, Sketches, Performances, Pantomimes and Shows written and/or performed in by Charles Kay

The Typical Topical Talker

Detective Copp

The House that Jack Built

Old Apple tree

The Pinks

Man in Blue

Sexton Blake

Do be Careful

Billy the Brokers Man

Babes in the Wood

A Dark Secret

The Dandy Boys

Kiss in the Ring

Cinderella

The Allies Musical

Colonel Percy

Robinson Crusoe

What Ho!

The Big Policeman and his Little Black Cat

The Simple Little Curate

Miss Paris in London

Little Babette

The Curate

The Colonel and the Yorkshire Lass

The Batchelor's Dream

You're spotted

Appendix lll

Songs written and/or performed by Charles Kay or one of his stage partners

'Love's request'

'I'm tired'

'Nursery Rhymes'

'A Tale of the Transvaal'

'I'm Off'

'I want to see the dear old house again'

'The beautiful tale of love'

'Come and Join the Territorial Army'

'Lucky Jim'

'Girls', Girls, Beautiful Girls'

'Nobody knows, nobody cares'

'Pussy had another Sardine'

'Same to you with knobs on'

'The new Humpty Dumpty'

'I know where the flies go'

'A muddled melody'

'We'll be welcoming the flies back'

'The twelve little maids'

'The 5.15' train'

Appendix IV

Newspapers, Journals and Magazines published between 1867 and 1928 that provided information for this publication

Exeter and Plymouth Gazette

The Western Times

The Daily Mail

Devon and Exeter Gazette

East & South Devon Advertsier

Evening telegraph

The Stage

The Era

The Throne and Country

The Whitstable Times and Herne Bay Herald

Dover Express

Taunton Courier

North Devon Journal

Teignmouth Gazette

Sussex Agricultural Express

Yorkshire Evening Post

Halifax Guardian

Nottingham Evening Post

Hull Daily Mail

New Devon Journal

The Western Morning News and Mercury, Australia

The Folkestone Herald

The Evening Post

Sussex Express

Folkestone, Hythe, Sandgate and Cheriton Herald

Morpeth Herald

Coventry Herald

Daily Herald, Australia

Surrey Express

Hartlepool Mail

Wells Journal

York Herald

Huddersfield Chronicle

Sheffield Daily Telegraph

Shields Daily Gazette

Manchester Courier and Lancashire General Advertiser

Derby Daily Telegraph

Sheffield Evening Telegraph

Index

Printed in Great Britain
by Amazon